NEPTUNE'S
ASYLUM

*Sea Stories
from the
1980s
U.S. Navy*

Kim Kipling

D1262225

Printed in the United States of America

First Printing, 2022

ISBN 979-8-9856393-2-2 (softcover)
ISBN 979-8-9856393-3-9 (ebook)

SharpenedEdge@protonmail.com

This book is dedicated to my beloved daughters Valerie and Kelly,
who were born while I was living these adventures, and who no doubt
often wondered why I was not there when they needed me to be.
It is also dedicated to my delightful grandchildren Will and Carrie
Beth. I hope my humble and undistinguished service has bequeathed
you a lifelong legacy of freedom and prosperity to pass along to your
own children. Given what is happening today in the Navy and indeed,
in America, that is far from certain, but I pray it will come to pass.
I love you all so very much.

CONTENTS

FOREWORD

I am a retired U.S. Navy Surface Warfare Officer. One of the great aspects of serving on Navy ships is observing the mayhem that sailors often create, intentionally or unintentionally, when they "get up to skippy." I have told a few of my favorite sea stories to friends over the years, and they often told me "you should write A BOOK of these." I decided that friends, family and other Navy veterans might enjoy hearing a few of the better ones, so began writing them down in my spare time. The stories took on a life of their own, and my pen was soon possessed by some unknown sea spirit with a mean streak and a wicked sense of humor. The project grew far beyond my initial plans. Friends I shared the written stories with insisted that I publish them (probably as irrefutable evidence of my inherently twisted nature.) So, sixty-plus chapters later, here we are at last. I submit my personal memories of the U.S. Navy of the 1980s for your reading enjoyment. Some are humorous, some are tragic, some are sobering. Each helps illustrate the borderline madness that was Sea Service in the waning years of the Cold War, as the winds of change blew and the insidious and ruthlessly applied forces of political correctness, diversity, equity and inclusion took root and worked their special brand of destruction on our beloved Navy. I weep for what was, and look at what is today with sadness and not a little disbelief. But let us not be troubled right now. Let's go back in time, to the era when *Miami Vice* ruled the TV ratings, the Space Shuttle *Challenger* was lost, the Berlin Wall fell, the Energizer Bunny made his debut and a band named Survivor sang *"Eye of the Tiger."*

Classic Navy question: "Do you know the difference between a sea story and a fairy tale?"

Answer: "A fairy tale begins 'Once upon a time...' A sea story begins 'Now, this is no sh$%...' "

Underway, shift colors. Sound one prolonged blast on the ship's whistle. All engines ahead full, rudder amidships. Steady as she goes.

Now, this is no sh$%......

"Kim Kipling"
LCDR, USNR (Retired)

M1911A1 .45 Pistol

CHAPTER 1

The Missing .45

In 1984, I was Communications Officer on board a guided missile cruiser, deployed to the western Pacific as Air Defense Coordinator (AW) of a Carrier Battle Group. The Commanding Officer (CO) of that ship (a Navy Captain, O-6) was a legendary screamer, who ruled by force and terror, and whose subordinate officers and men walked in fear of him with every step. He could and would arbitrarily ruin careers if anything happened to threaten his ambitions to ascend to flag rank. (This toxic leadership climate will figure prominently in future sea stories.) Well, demonstrative of the USN's short-sighted and flawed leadership culture, the terror strategy worked, and said CO was selected for promotion to flag rank. A new CO was selected and assigned to relieve the soon-to-be Rear Admiral, in port in Subic Bay, Philippines.

The ship is in port in one of a West Coast sailor's most cherished liberty ports. Adult Disneyland. The ship is being painted, and scrubbed from stem to stern. Uniforms are being pressed, brass polished, shoes shined. All accountable property is being inventoried, so a transfer of accountability can be made. This ship was (ahem) "nuclear capable", and had not one, not two, but three different launchers and magazines which (ahem) "could" contain nuclear weapons, so there was an extensive small arms inventory and guard force to look to their (ahem) "theoretical" security.

The ship's Weapons Officer **ordered** the Missile Officer (who was also the Small Arms responsible officer) to **personally** inventory all of the small arms. (This guy will also figure prominently in a future sea story.) 100% accountability of weapons is a VBD (Very Big Deal) in the Navy; losing one can end a career deader than a doornail. The Missile Officer took it upon himself to delegate this responsibility to a Chief Petty Officer (CPO), admonishing him to **personally** inventory the weapons. The CPO took it upon himself to delegate this responsibility to a First Class Petty Officer (PO1, E-6), admonishing him to **personally** inventory the weapons. The PO1 took it upon himself to delegate this responsibility to a PO2, admonishing him to **personally** inventory the weapons. Said E-5 actually did perform an inventory (I guess all the E-4s were busy scrubbing and painting and sweeping).......and found that a 1911A1 .45 ACP pistol was missing. This is incredibly bad juju. So.... he reports that all is well, all weapons present and accounted for. All hell is kept from breaking loose. Carry on smartly.

The Weapons Officer (an excellent officer and leader, by the way), knowing his men and what duty actually is, orders another Weapons Department officer who happens to be a Nuclear Engineer to spot check the small arms inventory. Wise move. Nukes ain't sloppy; checklists are God and orders are orders. A .45 pistol is quickly determined to be missing. The logbook shows it as last having been checked out several weeks earlier, at sea, during a weapons security drill. The signature / name in the logbook? "Irma Bombeck" (a popular newspaper columnist of the day.) **THIS PISTOL IS MISSING, HAS BEEN FOR SEVERAL WEEKS, AND THE SHIP IS IN PORT IN THE PHILIPPINES.** A bootleg .45 could be traded for days and nights worth of "adult recreation." The CO's shiny new stars, waiting in their satin-lined box, are in serious jeopardy of being revoked, and they are scheduled to be pinned on him in about 48 hours. Pandemonium ensues.

The crew of about 500 men is mustered at quarters. The Brow (gangway) is SECURED. No one is to leave or come onboard the ship. The entire 533-foot, 9600 ton ship is to be intensively searched, with nothing else to interfere. NO ONE IS DOING ANYTHING ELSE until the .45 is found. Period. Hours go by. The sun sets. Now remember, this is in Subic Bay, Philippines. Bar girls are weeping. Sailors are weeping. Even a few raging erections are weeping. The Brow remains secured, tempers are flaring and sweat is pumping like Niagara. Finally, one timid junior enlisted posits a question to the Command Master Chief: "if someone were to know something, could it just be turned in, no questions asked, no fault, no foul?" Thumbscrews are immediately (figuratively) applied, and a confession obtained. The .45 is recovered hidden, broken down into pieces and bolted under the deckplates of a storeroom deep in the bowels of the ship. The new "owner" had purchased it from another sailor, a PO1 who had checked it out during the drill and never checked it back in to the magazine. This gives probable cause to search the personal locker of the PO1, whose name is actually somewhat similar to "Irma Bombeck"... a simple, subtle substitution for the logbook which is likely not to be noticed. In the locker, the pistol belt, holster and magazine pouch from the .45 are found. Bam! Case closed.

In about 45 minutes, the thief is standing in front of the CO in dress whites. He had been a "frocked" E-6, meaning he was actually an E-5, but as he had been selected for E-6, he was allowed to wear the higher rank emblem. Instantly he is again an E-5. About 10 minutes later, he is an E-4, having been non-judicially reduced in rate for unauthorized retention of the belt, holster and mag pouch. He is frogmarched off the ship to the Brig in Subic, where he is subsequently tried by court-martial, convicted of the theft of the .45 and reduced in rank to E-3. He is given a sentence of several months incarceration, but allowed to remain in the USN. The CO is relieved of command on schedule, and wears his shiny new Rear Admiral's stars off the ship two days later as he is piped over the side. Peace reigns, unicorns gambol, and birds again sing.

Postscript: About a month later, the ship received a telegram from the Command Ombudsman back at home port. Apparently the tearful mother of a young infant wanted to know how the Navy could be so heartless as to let a new father volunteer for a "secret mission" which would prevent him from communicating, or returning home on schedule from deployment. I'm not sure how the Ombudsman broke the news to the grieving wife.

SSBN Deterrent Patrol Insignia

CHAPTER 2

Drugs and Neutrons Don't Mix

In 1979, I was honored to be one of the first four Third Class Midshipmen allowed to make our 3rd Class Mid Cruise onboard a Fleet Ballistic Missile Submarine. NROTC Midshipmen usually made three training cruises in the summers between their university years. The first of these cruises was made onboard a fleet unit, learning what an enlisted man's life is like. You lived in enlisted berthing spaces, performed junior enlisted duties and stood appropriate junior enlisted watches. You therefore learned what life is like "before the mast" and this experience should make you a better officer and leader in time. In my case, I was extremely interested in submarines, and had pestered my class instructor to inquire if I might not make my cruise aboard a boat, a *Benjamin Franklin*-class missile sub. A Nuke submariner, he somehow made it happen, and I was thrilled. I boarded an airplane for my very first flights, and traveled to Rota, Spain where I reported aboard my boat, USS GEORGE C. MARSHALL (SSBN-654). Shortly after I arrived, we were underway for a 64-day ballistic missile deterrent patrol. I quickly qualified at a few watch stations, and ultimately stood over 400 hours of watches at the helm and planes, literally driving the most potent weapon of war ever devised.

The late 1970s were not a good time to be in the US Navy in many ways. The decline and malaise of the Carter Presidency years was still very evident. Drug use and racial tensions were prevalent, and neither was good for discipline or morale. I was too busy marveling at the incredible precision and mechanical complexity of the submarine which was for the time being my home to think much about this. I slept in a bunk just outboard of an intercontinental ballistic missile, just about close enough to reach out and touch the launch tube. "Boomers" stay submerged and undetected when on patrol. "Slow, quiet and unknown" are the watchwords of daily life. I loved being aboard her. It was an interesting and eventful patrol in more than one way. I learned a lot. But one series of events was particularly instructive.

One day about halfway through the patrol, the Chief of the Boat (COB, who is the senior enlisted man aboard) was walking through the narrow passageway by the closed and locked door of the Corpsman's shack- the medical office of the boat, located on the middle level of the missile compartment. He smelled the unmistakable odor of burning marijuana. (Note: the air inside a submarine is recycled for days upon end. Smoke is readily apparent. It takes a special kind of dumbass to think that blazing up a joint is going to go unnoticed.) The COB followed his nose to the door, pounded on it and ultimately told whoever was inside that he was calling for a fireaxe and that the door was going to come open soon, one way or another. Sheepishly, the boat's corpsman (an HM1 E-6) opened the door, feigned having just awakened from a nap, and asked what all the fuss was about. The COB wasn't buying it. One rapid, glowingly positive urinalysis test later, it was clear that the HM1 had been smoking dope, and finding the ashes and spliff pretty much made it impossible to deny. Maximum pressure was then applied to the man concerning where he had obtained the drugs. He talked. Lockers were searched, based upon this probable cause, and other drugs were found. Pressure was applied. They talked. More searches were made. And ultimately, 12 men were found to be in possession of narcotics, all of whom tested positive for recent use. <u>This is over ten percent of the enlisted crew complement.</u>

Drug use was an instant disqualifier for possession of a security clearance in the USN, and by nature of their design, mission and operations, submarines are inherently highly classified. None of these men could, therefore, perform classified duties. They would be kicked out of the submarine service as soon as they could be gotten off the boat. Each knew that he had no future in the US Navy, at least not in submarines or classified ratings. And one of the men, an E-6 engineer, was one of three qualified nuclear reactor plant operators on the watch bill. He was instantly unable to even go aft of a certain door in the boat, to go anywhere near the reactor machinery. And the other two qualified reactor plant watchstanders immediately went on "port and starboard" watch – four hours on, four hours off, repeat.....for weeks. This is exhausting, and frankly, given the critical nature of that watch station, unsafe. Who wants a sleep-deprived, groggy man operating a nuclear reactor? No one anywhere near it, for sure.

The Captain (an incredible officer, who was both extremely knowledgeable and proficient, and an outstanding, inspiring leader) had a big problem. He could NOT pull his boat off of his ordered mission of ballistic missile deterrent patrol – this was a matter of utmost import to US national security. He could not call for permission to organize a mid-ocean rendezvous with a surface craft or helicopter, surface the boat, and offload the offenders and potentially take onboard new replacements. Surfacing meant certain detection, and likely compromise of the patrol. So, he had to keep the men aboard until the patrol ended.

Things went from bad to worse. Severe tensions arose between crew members. Some were angry at the dopers, especially the reactor plant operator, for having endangered their lives by getting high on patrol. Who wants a drugged man operating a nuclear reactor? No one anywhere near it, for sure! Mistakes and casualties can occur at any time on a boat, and proper, timely response is critical to mutual survival. Submarine crews must be on their best game at all times. The dopers were spreading the word to each other that they knew who had talked, and that revenge would be taken. Lives were threatened. And a couple of other crewmen who had not yet been ratted out and detected sent word to the ones who had been that if anyone talked about them, they would pay the penalty. This crew was literally tearing itself apart.

A deep funk of demoralization took over the boat, and watchstanding standards slipped markedly. Sailors were pretty much just "going through the motions" and coasting until the patrol ended. This is absolutely not what you want on this kind of boat, on patrol. And the Captain and COB needed to fix it, fast. The Captain gave a stern all-hands address to the crew, reading them the riot act and reminding them of Uniform Code of Military Justice (UCMJ) provisions that specified severe penalties for communicating threats, actual violence, or other infractions. He assured all that there would be zero tolerance for any further behavior of this sort, and application of the maximum penalties if it occurred.

This tamped down the fires but didn't erase the general malaise. So, one more step was taken. It was late one watch (missile submarines divorce themselves from celestial cycles when underwater. There is no midnight or noon, and only GMT observed. Day is night and night is day.) All was quiet. The COB quietly grabbed several off-watch sailors and bade them to come with him, each carrying several heavy steel weights which are used to make sure that ejected garbage from the boat doesn't float to the surface, to provide clues of presence and detection. The combined weight of men and steel was a few thousand pounds, and he walked them all the way to the torpedo room at the bow of the boat, upsetting her trim and making her very bow heavy, very quickly. The Captain, meanwhile, ordered the torpedo room to empty a torpedo tube, flood it, and fire a "water slug", or blank torpedo shot, into the sea, without reporting any of this to the control room. This results in a loud banging noise, a palpable jolt felt all through the boat, and a sudden whooshing of compressed air moving back through the boat rapidly. And then they hit the collision alarm, and reported "FLOODING IN THE TORPEDO ROOM!" **The combined effect of all of this was to give the very detailed simulated feeling of having collided with something forward, with a breach in the hull and the sea flooding in. And the boat was at patrol depth, far below the surface of the sea.**

You have never seen or heard the likes of the pandemonium that resulted. Orders flew. Depth and angle were sharply changed. Reports were made. Doors were slammed and dogged. Eyes were huge. Men were rushing to their assigned duty stations, many jolted awake from sleep. Some were audibly praying, and a couple were openly weeping. I was sitting at the helm, driving the boat, and I remember very clearly that this was the first time in my eighteen-year life span that I had ever faced death. I had a quick flash of great fear, and then, strangely, a calm resignation. I thought "you wanted to be here, doing this. There are worse ways to die than serving your country." And I felt no more fear after that. I will never forget the sensation. The boat was quickly brought under control. The drill was announced as having been just that, a drill. All was secured. And the COB and CO walked through each compartment from fore to aft, reminding every man that the sea never sleeps, and that they needed to be fully focused on their duties. They made their point. No man aboard likely ever forgot it again.

A few weeks later, the boat surfaced and transited into port in Holy Loch, Scotland. The boat was met by a pilot vessel and a harbor pilot. The hatch was opened, and normally, the first thing that happens is a bag of mail for the crew comes down the hatch, followed by the pilot. Not this day. The hatch opened, and twelve former submarine sailors were frogmarched up the ladder, and onto the pilot boat for transfer ashore, never to see the inside of a submarine again. Then down came the mailbag and the pilot, in that order.

The Captain made his point. And I proudly wore the SSBN Deterrent Patrol insignia for the remainder of my career, directly below my Surface Warfare insignia.

CHAPTER 3

Jerome

In 1987, I was Operations officer and Navigator of a Guided Missile Frigate. This class of ship had two helicopter hangars forward of a full-width helo deck, and a helo control booth overlooking the deck from high between the two hangars. Helo decks have numerous colored lights which are dimmable and also have a loudspeaker system so that the Helo Control Officer can issue directions to the deck crew even during noisy flight operations.

One of the new junior crew members on this ship was a very young sailor from inner city Detroit. He had never been anywhere outside his neighborhood before joining the USN and had only recently completed boot camp and been assigned to the Deck Division on my ship. Deck division performs deck seamanship tasks, handling mooring lines, anchoring, rigging refueling gear, and above all, painting the external areas of the ship. They stand watches as lookouts and helmsmen. This is where many non-technical sailors begin their shipboard training. Somehow he let slip to his division mates that he was scared of ghosts. Oops, bad idea. The other sailors in his division began referring to "Jerome" in his presence. When he asked who Jerome was, the other sailors told him that Jerome was a former crew member, who had died in his bunk during the last deployment, and had since been seen aboard the ship occasionally, haunting the passageways. They also informed the young lad that he, in fact was the new occupant of Jerome's old bunk and locker. Jerome was described as having been nasty-tempered and vindictive, and not too tolerant of new guys. This went on for some weeks.

When at sea, Navy ships are required to keep a visual watch at all times, pursuant to the International Rules for Prevention of Collisions at Sea (COLREGS). There are three lookouts; one on each bridge wing forward (port and starboard) and one all the way aft on the fantail. They are connected to the bridge by sound-powered telephones, and are tasked to report any relevant sightings of other ships, aircraft, weather, etc. The After Lookout is especially important, as part of his job is to listen and watch for any man overboard. If he doesn't see or hear a man overboard, the swimmer is likely to drown before recovery. A fundamental tenet of service is that NO ONE quits his post as a lookout without being relieved. NEVER.

One exceptionally dark night in the middle of the near-calm Pacific Ocean, I was standing a slow, uneventful watch as Officer of the Deck. The Bridge was pitch black, except for a few dim display lights needed for ship's control. I heard the Boatswains Mate standing Bridge Phone Talker watch call each lookout in turn for an hourly phone check. "Starboard Lookout, Bridge"..."Starboard Lookout , aye". Etc. Except this time, it was "After Lookout,

Bridge....After Lookout, Bridge....After Lookout, BRIDGE!" with no response. Young Seaman Apprentice Detroit is not answering the call.

The Boatswains Mate of the Watch sends a messenger to the fantail...who reports via the Sound Powered telephone that the after lookout is missing...he found the phones on deck, unattended. This is now a VBD (Very Big Deal.) Suddenly we realize that Seaman Apprentice Detroit is there, on the bridge, wedged into a gap between the chart table and the bulkhead, his back to the bulkhead, eyes wide, face ashen. When he is asked what he is doing there, instead of standing his watch on the fantail, he claimed to have been relieved at his post. By whom, we ask. Seaman Umptyfratz, he replies. "*Bull Sh%$!*", cries the Helmsman, none other than Seaman Umptyfratz!

So, what had happened is this: Seaman Apprentice Detroit had been standing watch all alone, on the fantail in pitch darkness in mid-ocean. One of the Boatswains Mates sneaked into the darkened helo control booth, brought up some dim red deck lighting and turned on the fantail loudspeaker with the volume low. He began pulsing the red deck lights using a rheostat control, giving a faint red glow which came and went, while whispering "*Jerooooooooooome......Jerooooooooooome...*" over the loudspeaker. Another sailor had donned a dark OD green rain poncho and was slowly walking back and forth across the tops of the helo hangars, barely visible as a spectral shape in the dim red intermittent light.

The sailor in the poncho swore that the kid was clear of the flight deck before the phones from his ears hit the steel of the deck......

The Shore Patrol

CHAPTER 4

"Sir? ME?" or Youthful Mistakes

Everyone has to start somewhere, I guess. And the Navy is a complex, unique culture with a lot of strange customs which high school does not prepare you to understand. My early learning curve was steep. I look back now and have to laugh at a couple of my youthful misadventures.

I. A lifelong dear friend and fraternity brother was a couple of years ahead of me in NROTC at my university. I was walking across campus one afternoon early in my freshman year, and ran across him, headed to the ROTC hangar building across the drill field from the main campus. He asked me if I was interested in pistol shooting. I had only ever fired two rounds from a tiny derringer owned by an early mentor, but as a true blue, red-blooded American male, I of course answered "YES!" He invited me to come along with him to pistol team practice. A lifelong love of the shooting sports was ignited that night, and I later became Captain of that NCAA Pistol Team. Tulane University also had pistol and rifle teams, and they sponsored an NROTC Invitational Rifle and Pistol Match every year, conveniently scheduled during Mardi Gras in New Orleans. This was, as you might imagine, a very popular event. The Navy supported it by assigning an Amphibious Transport vessel to dock at the foot of Canal Street in New Orleans, to provide no-cost berthing and meals for the competing midshipmen and their active duty coaches. Big berthing spaces normally full of Marines were an empty floating hotel, the ship's crew got to go to Mardi Gras, and everybody was happy with the arrangement.

My first year attending this match, the assigned ship was *USS FRANCIS MARION* (LPA-249). She was then quite aged, well past her prime, and the first active Navy ship I ever set foot on. I had been in my 4th Class Midshipman's uniform for about six months total. I reported aboard and took my modest luggage down to my assigned berthing compartment to get myself squared away and my bunk made. I looked around the compartment, found the head, and generally tried to acclimate myself to my strange new surroundings, in wide-eyed wonder. After a few minutes, the Commanding Officer was going ashore. His quarterdeck watch followed the ancient tradition of ringing the ship's bell and announcing his departure over the 1MC General Announcing system: (*ding ding...ding ding.* "FRANCIS MARION, departing".)

I couldn't run fast enough to find my way back topside to the quarterdeck and get off the ship. I thought she was getting underway, and I knew I wasn't supposed to go with her!

USS FRANCIS MARION (LPA-249)

II. On my first actual Midshipman Cruise (3rd Class Cruise), I was honored to be assigned to a ballistic missile submarine for a nuclear missile deterrent patrol. I had learned a lot by now...or so I thought. I reported to the Submarine Squadron staff aboard the submarine tender USS CANOPUS (AS-34) in Rota, Spain. The staff informed me that my boat was at sea on sea trials for a day or two, issued me and my fellow NROTC classmate an empty stateroom in officer's country aboard the tender, and told us where we could eat. They then left us alone, having much more on their minds than two wet-behind-the-ears 3rd Class Midshipmen to worry about.

Our uniform at that time was khaki shirt and trousers, with a thin gold chin strap on our combination covers (hats) and a tiny gold fouled anchor insignia worn on one collar point. At close range we looked as insignificant as we were. But at a distance, it was easy to mistake us for officers, given the khaki and gold colors. We decided to have a look around the ship, since we were off the chain of adult supervision. So we found our way topside and stepped out onto a metal walkway along the superstructure to enjoy the brilliant Spanish sunshine. We just happened to appear directly above an ongoing weapons handling evolution for another ballistic missile submarine of the squadron, berthed alongside the tender. Whenever a "boomer" is opening the accesses to tubes or magazines which contain nuclear weapons, a strict "exclusion area" is established, limiting access to those cleared and authorized personnel who are directly involved. This exclusion area is defined by and guarded by serious, no-BS, not-screwing-around US Marines, with real guns and live ammunition. And we had stepped into the exclusion area by going outside the skin of the ship onto that walkway.

A young Marine noticed us, and yelled *"Excuse me, sir, I need you to go back inside."* I took no notice, since as a 3rd Class Midshipman, no one had ever yet called me "sir."

A second challenge was issued, somewhat louder this time: *"EXCUSE ME SIR, I NEED YOU TO GO BACK INSIDE RIGHT NOW!"* My shipmate and I looked around, wondering who the young Marine was talking to! It certainly couldn't be us, in all our 18-year-old experience.

Suddenly, the Marine took it to another level. He chambered a round into his M16 rifle and looking directly into our eyes yelled *"Sir, GO BACK INSIDE THE SHIP IMMEDIATELY OR I WILL FIRE!"* We decided that we could clarify our rank and title information with the Marine at a later time, and scurried back into the ship where we belonged at maximum speed.

A "Boomer" loading a missile

III. A year later, I made my Second Class Midshipman's Cruise with several friends and classmates in a big gaggle of 19 year old officer trainees. This cruise exposed us to the various arms of the USN, to help us choose what part we wanted to serve in. We spent a week each with Aviation, Surface, Submarine and US Marine Corps units, getting a taste of what each does for a living. Submarine week was in Charleston, SC. After training was done for the day, we were allowed to go off base for liberty, so several of us of course did. Someone had heard that there was a great beach-side restaurant/club outside Charleston on the Isle of Palms, so we scraped up bus fare and headed in that direction. We met up with the daughters of a couple of local naval officers who were kind enough to show us around for an hour or so, and then split. (I guess we weren't as attractive as we might have hoped.) We stayed on the beach and tried to find some enjoyable trouble to get into, unsuccessfully. As it was getting late, we decided to head back to the Base. Uh Oh. The last bus for the night had already departed. And between us, we had nowhere near enough money left to hire a cab for the long ride back to the base.

One of my dearest friends and classmates is the son of a career naval aviator who had also commanded a Naval Air Station. He was familiar with the concept of a base having an "Officer of the Day" on duty. We scraped up a dime and placed a midnight call to the OOD, explaining our predicament. The bemused duty Lieutenant took pity on us and said he would send "the van" to get us. We were elated. We would make it back to morning muster on time and no keelhauling would take place. Woo hoo!

About 45 minutes later, up pulled "the van"...**the Shore Patrol van** used to take unruly sailors into custody and return them to the base brig. It had bars on the windows and no handles on the inside doors! Two uniformed Shore Patrol enlisted men were laughing fit to bust at having a gaggle of midshipmen to load into the back, and had us all sign a "non-custodial transfer" form indicating our consent to riding in the back of the USN paddy wagon. Of course we all signed, and rode back to base in a manner which I hope none of us ever experienced again. I know I never have.

CHAPTER 5

The Color Guard

Once in a while, major career events occur. In 1988, I was proud to organize the retirement ceremony for a remarkable shipmate. He was our ship's Command Master Chief, and also its First Lieutenant (Deck Division officer). This gentleman was a Master Chief Boatswain's Mate, a World War II, Korea and Vietnam veteran, and a former Navy Master Diver. He had spent a lifetime at sea on or under the water. (If you haven't seen it, the movie *Men of Honor* with Cuba Gooding, Jr. portrays what life as a Navy diver was like in the early days. It is worth watching.) He had served in many capacities, including as Command Master Chief of a huge amphibious assault ship with a crew of 900, plus 1700 Marines embarked for operations. At the twilight of his career, he had accepted orders to sea duty once more, on my comparatively small Guided Missile Frigate.

I wanted to send this incredible professional off right, honoring his many decades of service and at the same time recognizing his close association with the USMC. It's sad to say, but USN color guards can rarely compete for polish and precision with USMC color guards. And I wanted the best. So I called over to the USMC Recruit Depot (MCRD) in San Diego, and asked to speak with the officer-in-charge of the Base color guard. In time I was connected to a Marine 1st Lieutenant.

I explained what I was asking for. The Lieutenant then asked why the Naval Station San Diego color guard or a color guard formed by ship's company could not perform the task. I explained that I wanted "the best" – a USMC color guard. He paused, and then rather haughtily explained that "his Marines were not usually in the habit of supporting Navy ceremonies."

I replied: "Lieutenant, the Master Chief Boatswain's Mate I'm retiring is a World War II veteran. He took part in FIVE amphibious invasions in that war, serving in several of those as an assault craft coxswain. He's certainly done his part supporting the Marine Corps." (This was absolutely true.)

After a brief pause, The Devil Dog replied "Sir, what time and where would you like us to report?" And the Master Chief was piped over the side after a beautiful retirement ceremony featuring a razor-sharp USMC color guard.

ANZAC Day, 1985

CHAPTER 6

Worth It

In 1985, my Guided Missile Cruiser was deployed to the Indian Ocean. As we began our journey home, we were granted the holy grail of a Pacific sailor's port visits: Australia. While most of the battle group including the carrier visited Perth, my ship and a smaller Knox-class frigate made port in Geraldton, a smallish west coast city of about 30,000 located 260 miles north of there.

Aussies are extremely hospitable, friendly, and fun-loving. It is a totally unique landscape and culture. And while the younger generation of Australians have been infected with the socialist, politically correct claptrap of anti-freedom social justice warriors, older Australians are very pro-American. They remember, first and foremost, the Battle of the Coral Sea, and how America kept the Japanese from invading their vast and unprepared country. They fought alongside us in Vietnam and are the best international friends we have as a nation. Plus, they love their "beeah." My personal favorite was a local brew called Emu Export Lager. Delicious.

We were there over ANZAC Day, their version of our Memorial Day. It is a heartfelt remembrance of their staggering losses across two centuries supporting the military missions of the British Empire. They, quite rightly, take it seriously.

> *"They went with songs to the battle, they were young,*
> *Straight of limb, true of eye, steady and aglow.*
> *They were staunch to the end against odds uncounted,*
> *They fell with their faces to the foe.*
>
> *They shall grow not old, as we that are left grow old:*
> *Age shall not weary them, nor the years condemn.*
> *At the going down of the sun and in the morning*
> *We will remember them."*

from *For the Fallen*, by Robert Lawrence Binyon

I was proud to march, sword in hand, as Officer-In-Charge at the head of our ship's parade detachment, given a prominent place of respect in their town's memorial parade. And unexpectedly, for the rest of the port visit, I couldn't buy my own beer. I was treated with great hospitality.

One indication of how welcoming our Aussie "mates" were is the Dial-a-Sailor line. The phone company installed a telephone line on our ship's quarterdeck, and the town radio and TV stations publicized the number as widely as possible. A local wanting to host a visiting sailor merely had to dial the number. (Aussie accent) "Hiya, this is Sheila. My mate Cassie and I would like to meet two sailors! We'll be there about 6PM tonight, and we have a car...would that be all right?" Two lucky sailors' names would be assigned, and a date set. And then the phone would ring again..... Yes, the crew was pretty much in heaven.

One of the junior sailors of my department was a young Operations Specialist Seaman (E-3). OS's man the ship's Combat Information Center, or CIC. They operate radars, perform chart navigation and maintain displays of relevant battlespace data. The CIC is where a modern warship is fought from, not the bridge. This kid was excellent. He was tall, fit, good looking, maybe 19 years old. He had shown sufficient aptitude that he was already rated as an OS as an E-3. He was always on time, cheerful, diligent and smartly uniformed. He's the kind of kid you wish you had a dozen of. Early in the port visit, he had somehow hooked up with a stunning local girl. Petite, blonde, blue eyed, with a beautiful smile, a punky little gel-spiked hairdo, multiple pierced earlobes, and a smoking hot body. All coupled with that gorgeous Aussie accent. He was the envy of every shipmate. And we didn't see much of him whenever he was not on duty.

The sad day came when we had to depart. Liberty expired (that means the sailors were all required to return to the ship and resume duties) before sunrise, about 0500. The ship was scheduled to get underway at 0800. I happened to have the watch as Officer of the Deck on the Quarterdeck. And not long after, the Operations Division Senior Chief Petty Officer came to the Quarterdeck and informed me that the kid was missing. He had not returned to the ship and was now unauthorizedly absent. This is a punishable offense. It was also most unlike him. The ship began its detailed preparations for getting underway. This is a long series of actions and systems tests ensuring that all is ready, and then the actual procedures of undocking and driving away occur.

Time wore on. There was still no sign of the kid. This was becoming serious. It wouldn't be the first time that a young sailor had fallen in love and decided to desert the Navy and marry the girl of his dreams. (It never ends well. Sooner or later, one is apprehended and brought to account. I once saw a man in civilian clothes, in his late 40's returned to our ship. He had deserted from her over twenty years earlier, and had recently been arrested for something, and his outstanding warrant had come to light. We held him for a few hours until he could be transferred ashore and a court-martial arranged.) And if this desertion happens overseas, the man is at the same time instantly an illegal alien in the country where he has deserted. Everybody wants him, and not in a good way. He's in a heap of trouble. A court-martial conviction for desertion is a federal offense, never to be blotted from a man's record. And we genuinely hated to see this good kid go down that road to ignominy.

The checklist of preparations continued. One item required to be tested is the ship's whistle, a loud horn which conveys maneuvering signals to other ships in the event of fog or risk of collision. In our case, this was a deep, stentorian, steam-powered behemoth. It was, by design EXTREMELY LOUD.

BRRRRRRRRRRRRRRRRRRP! went the whistle. And at the far edge of the parking lot next to the ship, there was an explosion of activity in the back seat of a parked car. Out popped the missing kid, pulling on his shirt and hopping into his shoes, hotfooting it to get aboard before we pulled the brow and left him behind. The little Aussie girl was hanging on him, tears flowing. One more goodbye kiss, and he flew up the brow into the waiting arms and stern expression of his Senior Chief. He was asked what had happened, and explained that he had wanted to make absolutely sure that he was on time, so he had asked the girl to drive him to the ship by 0430 – half an hour early. A goodbye hug and kiss had gotten steamy....and turned into one last interaction in the back seat of her car, where both had apparently fallen asleep in rapturous entanglement. And only the ship's whistle had waked them up, moments before.

The Senior Chief gave him a preliminary chewing out (as only a CPO can do!) , making sure he knew that his very life was in jeopardy, and that at the very least **he would be performing extra duties for the rest of his Navy career. HE MIGHT EVEN BE KEELHAULED, IF THE SENIOR CHIEF CONTINUED IN HIS BAD MOOD FOR A DAY OR TWO!** The kid's head hung progressively lower and lower. Finally, the Senior Chief looked him over, and said "I just have one question.....was she worth it?"

The young sailor's head came up, and a beatific smile came instantly to his face. In a voice of pure, honest elation he replied "Oh, YES, Senior Chief!" He was curtly dismissed and sent below to don his dress whites preparatory to manning the rail as we departed.

And the Senior Chief and I managed to keep straight faces and not explode into laughter until he was out of earshot.

SM-2 ER missile

CHAPTER 7

Douching a Surface-to-Air Missile

My first ship was an 9600+ ton steam-powered Guided Missile Cruiser. After a year-long baseline overhaul, countless inspections and systems certifications and pre-deployment workups, it was in its homeport of San Diego just a few days before deploying to the Indian Ocean as Air Defense Coordinator (AW) of a Carrier Battle Group.

This class of ship was armed with the Standard Missile -2, Extended Range (SM-2ER) surface to air missile system. These missiles were huge two-stage affairs, which could shoot down enemy aircraft or missiles at long range (we once got a skin-to-skin hit on a target drone at 89 nautical miles...good shooting!) Think supersonic flying telephone poles with explosive warheads.

The missiles were housed in two separate missile magazines, one each fore and aft. Each magazine had two huge revolving circular racks of 20 missiles each, resting more or less horizontally. Behind each missile's rocket motor was a booster suppression system. The BSS was seawater under pressure, with a nozzle positioned such that if a missile's rocket motor lit off in the magazine, it would shatter a frangible burst disk in the nozzle and allow the high-pressure water to jet up the missile's rear, inhibiting (but not extinguishing) the rocket exhaust fire and theoretically preventing a catastrophic missile magazine fire and explosion.

On this soon-to-be-less-than-peaceful day, the ship's Missile Officer (who figured prominently in an earlier Sea Story (#1 *The Missing .45*) was having an argument with his Division's Leading Chief Petty Officer. To keep from "arguing in front of the kids", they took the "discussion" below decks in the missile magazine. Now, this officer had one major qualification for a stellar USN career: he had played football at the Naval Academy. He was a pretty stout guy, physically.

So at some point, to underscore his argument, the Missile Officer slammed his hand down onto a booster suppression nozzle. And...BOOM, the burst disk did its thing, and high pressure seawater went shooting up the back end of a Standard Missile, spraying saltwater all over all of the other birds in the compartment. Pandemonium reigned for a brief time. The proper valve was shut, the seawater was pumped out of the magazine, and massive effort was made to carefully hand-dry and corrosion-treat the remaining 39 birds, hoping that their sensitive electronics had not been damaged. But the one missile was undoubtedly dead as a doornail.

This is now a major problem. A major combatant like this ship simply did not deploy with an empty weapon rack, much less one with a dead missile in it. Calls were made. The two weapons handling berths within reasonable range were both scheduled for other ships; booked solid for a couple of weeks. Discussions began concerning having a sister ship of the same class deploy as Air Defense Coordinator for the battle group, with our ship following behind and "taking back over" once we caught up. (In reality, the other ship would likely have been allowed to keep the premier job.) Now, our Captain was senior to the other ship's CO, and was directly competing with him for selection to flag rank. There was no way in hell he was going to play second fiddle. None. Period. More calls were made and favors called in or promised.

The next day, the forecastle was secured. The Missile Division was mustered on the forecastle for a weapons handling detail. A portable crane drove up the pier and set up operation. And in port, pierside in downtown San Diego, a Mike Boat landing craft pulled alongside WITH A LIVE SM-2 MISSILE ABOARD. (In case you are wondering, this is dangerous, strictly forbidden by regulations, and pretty much unprecedented. Imagine the national news coverage if a mishap were to occur.) Old missile was craned off. New missile was stowed below decks, joining its siblings without befalling disaster. And the ship deployed on schedule, with a full magazine of birds. And the careers of all concerned continued without interruption. I guess safety rules were made to be broken when an ambitious officer's promotion is at stake.

CHAPTER 8

Mooring To A Buoy

My ship, a 445-foot, 4200 ton Guided Missile Frigate, was returning to the USA in 1987 after an eventful deployment to the Persian Gulf. We were ordered to proceed to Hong Kong for a well-deserved and much anticipated port visit. We transited the South China Sea, passed Lei Yu Mun, and proceeded to our assigned berth, a buoy mooring in Victoria Harbor.

Now, mooring to a buoy can be a bit tricky, as the technique is not that often used by USN ships. Basically, a stout nylon mooring hawser with an eye splice in the end is passed through the bow fairlead (aka the "bullnose") and dropped to a small boat, which takes it over to the firmly-anchored buoy. An intrepid seaman climbs aboard the buoy, and attaches the hawser to a mooring ring with a large screw shackle. The shackle pin is screwed into place and moused with wire as a safeguard to prevent its unscrewing and letting the ship go adrift. Presto, you are moored. In theory.

This day, conditions were a bit challenging. Winds and current were making it hard to keep the bow of the ship near the buoy. The assigned seaman was struggling to stay aboard the spinning buoy, attach the shackle and complete the rig. Finally, all was completed and the boat stood clear. The trouble was that the bow was still too far from the buoy. So, the mooring hawser was taken to power at the capstan, and placed under tension to shorten it up.

Every sailor at some point is made aware of the extreme danger posed by nylon mooring lines placed under extreme tension. They stretch, like rubber bands, and if they part or are suddenly released, they can literally cut a man in half. Or several men. A graphic training film made in the 1970s amply illustrated this, using mannequins dressed in navy uniforms subjected to a parted mooring line. Bodies and limbs flew around like matchsticks, and no sailor who ever saw this film ever forgot it.

Having navigated the ship to the assigned berth, my duties as Navigator were complete, and I was watching the forecastle mooring detail, interested because these were sailors of my Operations Department. In charge on the forecastle was my First Division officer, a World War-II veteran Master Chief Boatswain's Mate. He had forgotten more about deck seamanship than I'll ever know. I certainly wasn't shouting down helpful corrections from the bridge wing. The mooring hawser stretched...and stretched...and stretched some more. It was bar tight. Still the ship's head resisted coming into the wind and closing on the buoy. Suddenly, the men tailing the hawser as it ran off the capstan somehow allowed a riding turn or two to surge over the top of the capstan, instantly releasing the tension on the hawser. The hawser snapped back to its resting length. It sounded like a pistol shot. Several men lost their feet and hit the deck. And I clearly saw a mist cloud appear at the right calf of one man hit by the surging line. I thought: that's it. Several guys are dead or severely injured. I think my heart stopped.

Slowly, everybody got to their feet. Even the man whose leg had been hit. He had a two-inch hole friction burned through his dungaree trousers and a first-degree rope burn on his calf. The mist cloud I saw had been smoke, not blood. A few others had some bruises or scrapes; that was it. We had been extremely lucky. Work resumed, mooring was completed, and the crew enjoyed an excellent port visit.

I think my heart restarted sometime during the next watch.

Forecastle Line Handlers

"Permission to come aboard"

CHAPTER 9

Quarterdeck Traditions

One of the U.S. Navy's greatest strengths is its unique traditions. Tracing most of these cultural heritage touchstones back to the British Royal Navy and many to even earlier centuries, our Navy enjoys a rich historical legacy of nautical customs. They are what makes a navy a navy rather than just another land-based service with a slightly different uniform. Almost everything about sea service is informed and shaped by the environment and long historical custom. This is why naval uniforms and rank titles are so different from other services'.

Nowhere is this echoing reflection of ancient traditions more apparent than on the Quarterdeck. The Quarterdeck is the ceremonial and official entrance to the ship when in port. It has for centuries been a place of respect bordering on reverence.

Decorum is observed in behavior and speech. Officers and visitors come aboard there. It is customary to salute twice when doing so, first rendering a smart hand salute to the national ensign flying astern, and secondly saluting the quarterdeck itself, by rendering a hand salute to the Officer of the Deck, no matter his rank. One then requests permission to come aboard, rather than just assuming it and stepping on. This custom reflects a bygone time when ships carried religious icons on their quarterdecks, with the crew often paying reverent respect to them as a matter of invoking the benevolent protection of the gods against a lethal environment. It paid to keep the almighty powers on your good side, so that they might stand between you and storm, lightning, wind and sea, starvation, disease and occupational hazard. Over the centuries, this became a customary reverence towards the Quarterdeck itself. Watches are stood there in dress uniform vice working wear. It is kept in a high state of order and cleanliness, and it is often elaborately decorated with nautical fancywork.

Senior officers coming aboard was and is a big deal. The ship's reputation (and coincidentally that of her Captain) is reflected by the appearance of the Quarterdeck, and the correctness of the Quarterdeck watch's procedures. It was important to have as much advance warning of the approach of a senior officer who rated ceremonial honors as possible, to give time to prepare to look your best and do things right. For that reason, the Officer of the Deck was by regulation supposed to have a spyglass at hand, to improve his far vision. Yes, a spyglass. Not binoculars, these had not yet been invented. At least when I was on active duty, USN ships still had spyglasses in inventory for use on ceremonial occasions. Many is the formal quarterdeck watch I have stood with one nestled in the crook of my left arm, where it did not interfere with my right hand salute.

Nowadays, OSHA-approved brows, or gangways, make it easy to come aboard safely. This was not always the case. Back in the days of sail, wooden steps led up the side of the ship and had to be climbed, sometimes against the ship's motion and varying hull curvature, in all weathers. Men could and did fall occasionally. Senior officers coming aboard were particularly important. It simply would not do to have a Captain or Admiral killed or injured, or even made to look foolish by encountering trouble when coming aboard. The more senior the officer, the more likely he was to be obese, handicapped due to long service in a profession where malnutrition, dehydration, and combat injury were common, or suffering the infirmities of advancing age. It was a good idea to have a few hands available to help them get up the side and through the bulwark gangway. So when a senior officer approached, a few able men were tasked to help them. These are known as Sideboys, and they are always paraded in pairs, one on either side of the entrance gangway. The officer came aboard and passed between them. If he needed a little help getting aboard, they were there to help on both hands. The number of Sideboys reflects the seniority of the officer concerned. A Commanding Officer holding the rank of Lieutenant Commander or below rates two Sideboys. A Commander or Captain rates four, a Commodore or Rear Admiral six, and a Vice Admiral or Admiral eight.

When the officer concerned is seen approaching the gangway, the ships bell is rung in sets of two strokes, matching the number of Sideboys the officer rates. On ceremonial occasions, a Boatswain's Mate pipes a specific call on his boatswain's pipe, which again features flourishes dependent upon seniority. And an announcement is made giving the officer's command title (if held) or at least their rank.

So the whole process might look like this. The Commanding Officer of USS GRIDLEY wants to come to visit your CO to congratulate him on his change of command ceremony which is taking place that day aboard your ship. Full ceremonies are in effect. The Quarterdeck watch is stationed in dress uniforms, with as many as eight Sideboys and a Boatswain's Mate standing by. The Officer of the Deck, holding a spyglass, sees him approaching, identifies him, and determines that he holds the rank of Commander, so he is entitled to four Sideboys. He orders the ship's bell rung four times, in two sets of two, and makes an announcement over the ship's general announcement PA system: "(*ding ding...ding ding*) GRIDLEY, arriving."

Four Sideboys step up to flank the gangway, at attention. The visiting officer salutes the ensign, then the Officer of the Deck and says "request permission to come aboard".

The OOD returns his salute and says "Welcome aboard, sir" The Boatswain's Mate blows his call as befits the officer's rank as the officer steps aboard and passes between the Sideboys. (This is called being "piped aboard.)" The visiting officer is undoubtedly met by a ship's officer and respectfully conducted to the CO if he doesn't come meet him personally. And that centuries-old practice is still conducted today, with precision and pride reflecting our unique sea service.

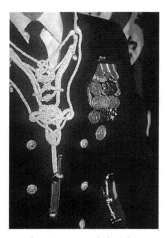

The Boatswain's Pipe

P.S.: What's with the Boatswain's Pipe, or "Call" as it is sometimes referred to? This is an archaic form of whistle, made of a non-corrosive metal, which has no moving parts. It was used to make several differing specific calls, or tunes, if you will, which had specific meanings related to orders or procedures. On a ship powered by the wind, with the ever-present sound of wind and sea, it could be heard and understood more readily than the human voice when conditions were harsh. It was worn on a lanyard about the neck of the Boatswain's Mates, and only used by them to relay orders to men aloft, on and below decks. Over the centuries, it became a ceremonial badge of office for Boatswain's Mates, and they are still entitled to wear it in dress uniform.

USS TAURUS (PHM-3)'s Anchor

CHAPTER 10

Steel Vs. Aluminum. Steel Wins.

My last ship was a *Pegasus*-class Guided Missile Hydrofoil. These incredible ships were unique and remarkable. 132 feet long, with a complement of 5 officers and 19 enlisted men, they could poke along hullborne at about 10 knots or less, or, under jet turbine power, they literally flew at speeds in excess of 50 knots, with the hull completely out of the water, supported on stainless steel hydrofoil "wings". They were armed with eight Harpoon anti-ship guided missiles and a 76mm automatic gun. They punched way above their weight and were extremely potent weapons in the anti-ship role. Design-wise, they were a hybrid of ship and aircraft design, and they were built of aluminum for weight reasons.

In 1989, my ship was operating foilborne in the Western Caribbean Sea on a counter-narcotics mission. It was a very rough night, with seas of 8-10 feet and winds over 25 knots under completely overcast skies. In conditions like that, the ship's motion was a bit like a runaway subway train; very little roll, slight yaw, but a rapid, plunging pitch as the forward foil tried to maintain a set depth below the large, cresting waves. It was the middle of the night and I was semi-asleep in my bunk. Foggily, I awoke to several very loud banging noises. It sounded exactly like a fifty-caliber M2 machine gun firing single shots, topside. Just as I asked myself "what the hell are we firing a Ma Deuce at, foilborne, on a night like this?" I realized...."We don't HAVE a Ma Deuce!"

The ship suddenly landed as I rolled out of bed, threw on my uniform and shoes, and rushed to the bridge. As I got there, reports began coming in of flooding in several forward compartments. Not long after that, reports came forward of 1/2" of jet fuel (our main propulsion fuel) on deck in the officer's bunkroom, where a large fuel tank sat directly under my bunk. This was not good.

A brave E-5 electrician went below into a partially-flooded storeroom to secure an electrical switchboard and try to ascertain the cause of the flooding. He reported several gashes through the hull, freely communicating with the ocean. Another engineer located the source of the jet fuel – the sounding tube for that tank, which had not been tightly capped, and secured it, stopping the jet fuel flow into the ship. We quickly pumped out the fuel on deck. Things were stable for the moment. I am pleased to say that the superb crew of this ship each acted with icy calm and complete professionalism in crisis. Bravo Zulu, guys.

This class of ship was fitted with a 150-lb steel Danforth anchor, with a short length of steel chain and a long nylon mooring hawser. The anchor was kept in its hawsed (stowed) position on deck by a holdback bar clamping it down. About 75 feet of hawser was usually faked out on deck for immediate use if needed, with the rest coiled on a locking reel against the superstructure's forward face. In the rough weather, a corroded component of the holdback bar broke, and the anchor fell over the side, paying out the hawser until the locked reel stopped further line from unreeling. Then, the steel anchor, being dragged along and through rough seas at 50 knots on the end of a long elastic line, began slamming into the aluminum underhull of the ship, which was of course above the water as we were foilborne. Nine or ten impacts had left 14 breaches of the hull, including our main fuel tank. When we landed, in came the water. It filled up the fuel tank from the bottom, with the lighter fuel floating on the heavier seawater, and flowing out of the loosely-capped sounding tube into the ship.

We got as much secured as possible, were released from our mission, and directed to proceed to Colon, Panama for temporary repairs. Had we done so hullborne, this would have been an excruciating transit of more than three days in rough seas. We naturally went foilborne at high speed for a few hours. The only issue was, now the water-contaminated fuel tank was leaking back into the sea due to gravity.....and we needed that fuel. Our engineers looked at the logbooks to determine what amount had been in the tank before the incident. When enough of the heavier water had drained out and we felt that what remained in the tank was mostly fuel, we began to transfer as much fuel as possible, as rapidly as possible, to other tanks via fuel purifiers. We saved as much as we could and made it back to port in Panama with a comfortable margin for safety.

Okay, this is where things get interesting. We were assigned a remote berth in Colon. It would take the local SEAL Team detachment a day or two to weld temporary patches over our holes, to enable us to get back to the USA for permanent repairs. Tensions in Panama were very high. The Panamanian dictator

Manuel Noriega was still in charge, and his "Panamanian Defense Force" thugs pretty much had free rein. A jeep full of them appeared at the end of our pier, sporting dirty wife-beater t-shirts, blue jeans, and AK-47s. They made a point of spitting, giving us the finger and cursing at us, pretty much all day. This had me concerned. Navy ships at that point were customarily guarded by a single enlisted man, the Petty Officer of the Watch, wearing an unloaded .45 pistol in a flapped holster, with two five round magazines in a flapped magazine pouch. That is what the USN called security, and it was pathetic. I walked up to the bridge and found my ship's only Gunner's Mate on watch, in dress whites as specified by regulations, with his unloaded .45. This excellent sailor was an E-6 (First Class Petty Officer). He was a South Philly Italian, named Carmine, and he was intensely practical. The ship was lucky to have him.

Looking up the pier at Noriega's finest, I said "Gunner, maybe we should bring a 12-gauge shotgun up here, just in case." He looked at me with a curious expression and then asked "XO, would an M14 rifle do?" I said "Sure, even better." And without another word, he reached behind the ship's control console and pulled out an M14 and a full bandolier of magazines and set it against the console where it was ready to hand. He looked at me with a smile on his face. I said "Gunner, that's what we pay you for." (Had I objected to his removing the weapon from the armory without permission, he had also brought along cleaning gear, and his excuse was going to be " I was taking advantage of my watch to clean it." Smart guy. Gotta love a good NCO.)

Later that day, I called for a jeep to take me to the US Army base dental clinic, as I was having a dental problem and they said they could fit me in. The driver took an unusual route to the Base clinic, passing through deserted housing areas, with empty homes, silent playgrounds, motionless swing sets, and no activity whatsoever. All personnel had been evacuated. We stopped at a stop sign, and I looked over into the vegetation at the road intersection's edge...

and made eye contact with a wide-eyed young US soldier, in full battle dress and face camo, with an M249 SAW with a belt of live ammo loaded in the feed tray!

Now I'm not the smartest guy in Panama on that day, but even I can tell this is not normal. The driver ain't saying anything. Neither are the dental technicians. I got my tooth fixed, and returned to the ship. We got patched up, and sent on our way as quickly as the local base could arrange it. And while we were in transit back to Key West, FL, Operation *Just Cause*, the US invasion of Panama, took place. We had not been part of it, had not been told about it, and were simply gotten out of the way of it.

I hope the PDF thugs got what was coming to them during the festivities. A great friend and co-worker of mine is a retired Army Sergeant Major, and a veteran of several elite special operations units. He combat parachuted into Rio Hato airfield that night. He assures me that they did.

PHMs in flight

The NAS Cubi Point "O" Club Bar

CHAPTER 11

The Last Beer

In late 1994, I was posted to the U.S. Embassy in Manila, Philippines. I was still a Naval Reserve officer at the time, as I had not yet retired. This was a time of great upheaval in the US Navy presence in the Far East, as the Philippine Senate had voted to eject US forces from their bases in the country. Several major bases were closed, and all US military personnel departed the country.

One of these bases was NAS Cubi Point. The officer's club at NAS Cubi Point was the site of a legendary bar. It was well known and beloved to thousands of officers who enjoyed R&R there, especially during the Vietnam War. The walls were covered with hundreds of squadron plaques and other memorabilia of decades of deployments, many in direct combat. If you have ever seen the 1991 movie *Flight of the Intruder*, a major scene is set in the Cubi O-Club bar. Yes, many inebriated patrons did in fact simulate carrier landings in a contrived "trap" apparatus, with a dunking in a pond at the end if you missed catching the arresting wire. From a recent website posting describing the place:

> *"Oh my goodness! There never was any Officer's Club like the Cubi Pt. one, nor will there ever be again. The wild escapades of naval officers and aviators letting off steam following their long periods at sea and especially in combat are the stuff of legends. Oh, the many stories the still standing but long closed building's walls could tell."*

I had visited the club while on active duty in 1984, 1985 and again in 1987, during deployment port visits. It had a majestic view, inexpensive drinks, and a wild and well-earned reputation for debauchery. It was an unforgettable experience.

One day in late 1994, my work took me to the recently-closed NAS Cubi Point. All American personnel were gone, the base was under Philippine control, and it was basically a ghost town. I drove by the O-Club for old times' sake. The door to the O-Club was standing open! Of course, I had to stop in to reminisce. The place was pretty much deserted, but a table by the front door had a few odd pieces of the Club's dining room china sitting on it, with a sign indicating that they were for sale. I called around until I found a nice Filipino gentleman cleaning up the place and asked if I might still buy a souvenir or two. "Of course!" he replied, and I did. I asked if I might walk about the place for old time's sake. "No problem, sir!" I walked back to the bar. There it was, with all those colorful plaques still on the wall, echoes of nights past, warriors fallen and alive whispering across decades. Empty boxes sat on the floor, and the gentleman indicated that the memorabilia was to be removed and packed into them, for transport back to the USA. The dust was settling on what had been a vibrant, intense epicenter of naval tradition and lore. The silence reigned over the red leather chairs and barstools, the music system turned off, the band stage empty.

I asked the gentleman, "Do you happen to have any beer, still? He indicated that he did. "Would you sell me one?" I asked. "Sure, sir!" he cheerfully replied. I laid a few dollars on the bar, and the gentleman opened a cold bottle of San Miguel beer from the small refrigerator behind the bar and set it in front of me.

And that is how a Surface Warfare Officer, not an aviator, drank the last beer in the NAS Cubi Point Officer's Club bar.

Postscript: The NAS Cubi Point Officer's Club bar has been recreated, using those original plaques and other artifacts, and is today the visitor's café at the National Naval Aviation Museum in Pensacola, Florida. I hope to visit it again someday.

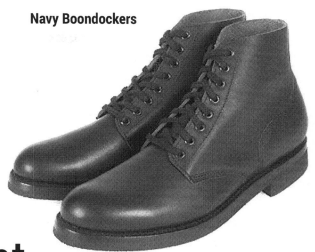

Navy Boondockers

CHAPTER 12

Midnight Passageways and a "Hostile Leadership Climate"...Really!

In 1984, my ship was undergoing Refresher Training (REFTRA) in preparation for a 7-month deployment to the Western Pacific and Indian Ocean. The ship was a steam-powered 533-foot, 9600 ton guided missile cruiser, commanded by a Captain (O-6) and with a crew of approximately 500 men. The Commanding Officer was a legendary "screamer", who had a notorious reputation for abusive leadership and who harbored a limitless ambition for promotion to flag rank. This guy was going to be an admiral, come hell or high water, and woe to anyone who he perceived as standing in his way in any manner, great or small.

One peculiar aspect of this Captain's leadership philosophy was his absolute insistence that the ship look her COSMETIC best at all times. Appearance was the most important aspect of life aboard this ship. (I later learned that this idea was directly cribbed from a 1956 movie, *Away All Boats*, starring Jeff Chandler and featuring a very young Clint Eastwood in a bit part.) "Run she may, but shine she must" was the mantra of this philosophy, modified slightly by our CO to "Run she will, but shine she must" – he was fully willing to demand both his cake and the privilege of eating it too.

There were lots of manifestations of this philosophy put into action on this ship, but probably the most stark example was the ship's routine of "Midnight Passageways." Now, this was a major combatant warship; first and foremost a fighting vessel, packed with men, machinery and weapons and intended to seek out and destroy enemies. It is an industrial environment, characterized by close quarters, much to do and much to practice and maintain in order to be able to fulfil that role. There was plenty to keep the men occupied with meaningful work and training. But that stuff won't get you your admiral's stars....APPEARANCE will. So the Captain demanded that every bulkhead of every passageway on the ship be painted in gloss white enamel. Every deck was tiled in royal blue linoleum tile. No black vinyl baseboards intended to hide shoe scuffs and other evidence of firehoses, machinery or heavy traffic were allowed. Shiny white paint extended down to shiny waxed blue tile, and a bead of shiny white caulk ran down the seam where the two met. This, in every passageway through the entire ship.

To maintain this pristine environment of stunning beauty, the Captain mandated "Midnight Passageways" details. This meant that every night in port, on the midnight watch when most of the duty section was asleep, a senior petty officer mustered a working party totaling a dozen or so junior enlisted men representing each

Division, who proceeded to strip, wax and buff the deck of every single passageway aboard the ship. They also had to apply touch up paint to any dings in the bulkhead enamel which might have appeared through the day. Every. Single. Night. Then, when all was complete and the shiny new floor wax was dry, the First Class Petty Officer (E-6) inspected each passageway. He then awoke a Chief Petty Officer (E-7/8/or/9) who then inspected each passageway, to ensure it had been polished sufficiently. And ultimately, a junior officer had to perform an inspection when summoned by the CPO. By about 0400 or so, the process would be completed, unless immediate corrective action needed to be taken.

All of this was but prelude. At about 0600, the ship's Executive Officer (XO, or second-in-command, in this case a Commander (O-5)) arrived onboard, ensuring that he arrived well before the Captain. The XO had to be met on the Quarterdeck upon his arrival by the First Class Petty Officer from the night before, and they together walked through and inspected every single passageway. And if things were not sufficiently shiny to the XO's satisfaction, there was immediate hell to pay. The Officer and CPO whose passageway was the offender would be immediately summoned, chewed out publicly and singled out for verbal abuse and humiliation on the spot. This then flowed downhill to all concerned below them. In time, as the Captain's screening board for promotion approached, the XO's abusive conduct ratcheted up even further. He began to actually lay hands on sailors; shoving them, jacking them up against bulkheads, cursing at them, manhandling them, when real or imagined deficiencies were noted in the passageways shined at midnight by tired, sleep-deprived, dispirited sailors with too much to do as it was. Now, striking an officer is a very serious offense under the Uniform Code of Military Justice (UCMJ), so these men were basically powerless to defend themselves. He knew this, hid behind his rank, and abused them with impunity.

Needless to say, unpunished crime begets further transgression. Things came to a head during Refresher Training. For those who do not know, REFTRA is the most intense and difficult period in a ship's life, short of actual battle damage. For a period of 4-6 weeks, a team of trainers and inspectors come aboard, and put the ship through an extensive series of drills, grading each one and noting both performance and material deficiencies. The standards are extremely demanding. Drills are intense, and go on all day and all night, in port and at sea. Sleep deprivation is a way of life. And careers can be ruined if the ship does poorly. Captains and Engineers and other officers can be summarily relieved. It is a very stressful and difficult process.

One night, late at night in REFTRA, the ship was called to General Quarters. That means "battle stations" for a drill, with each man reporting to his battle station. It became apparent that the drill of the moment was focused on engineering. So many of these men were completely superfluous to the situation, had no role in standing the current watch, and were simply awake and standing by for no reason. I was the Communications Officer, and responsible for the Radiomen and Signalmens' divisions. I was not there to witness what happened next, but was told in great detail by several eyewitnesses.

My Radio Compartment was full of all of the ship's radiomen. Several had watch duties, several did not, and had been awakened just to go to General Quarters. So one of my E-6 Radiomen (who had no current role to play and who had to be rested and performing well in just a few hours when it was his turn to stand watch as a radio supervisor) found a spot out of the way between several racks of radio equipment, laid down on deck and went back to sleep. I have no problem with this; fatigue management is a POSITIVE skill for a combat leader. Having some men rested for later duties is a useful mission factor.

Something brought the XO into Radio. He was already very agitated about something. And he spied the sleeping E-6. He flew into a rage, ran over and began KICKING THE SLEEPING MAN, hard, in the ribs and gut, with what were described to me as full force, field-goal, soccer penalty kicks. He was frothing at the mouth, spitting curses and hurling abuse on the man while landing pedal haymakers. And then he departed.

The ship returned to port the following day, undertook some material maintenance and repairs, and then got back underway in about 18-24 hours. And when the ship got underway, the assaulted E-6 Radioman did not report aboard, and missed the ship's movement. This is a major infraction under the UCMJ, and the Radio Chief Petty Officer reported his absence to me immediately. Efforts to contact the man ashore failed. And while the ship was at sea this day, it received a message from the Surface Forces Pacific (SURFPAC) Public Affairs Officer. SURFPAC had been contacted by the *San Diego Union* newspaper, who were investigating a report they had been given that a ship's officer had assaulted an enlisted man aboard the ship. SURFPAC wanted to know what to tell the *San Diego Union*.

A private conference was called with the CO, the XO, and my department head, the Operations Officer. A brief cable was sent back to SURFPAC, saying only that the matter was "being investigated", thereby buying time. The ship returned to port that afternoon on schedule.....and was met by the missing E-6 Radioman, who was standing on the pier. He had already told several shipmates that he was severely bruised and had been urinating blood, before he missed movement. He had a pensive, resigned look on his face. The Operations Officer met the man on the quarterdeck, and immediately escorted him directly to the Captain's cabin, where the door was shut in my face. As his Division Officer, I should have been included in any and all conversations with the man, but I was not. After about 20 minutes, the Radioman came out, went directly to his locker, and packed all his uniforms and other belongings. He was reluctant to speak to any of his shipmates. But he did tell his Chief Petty Officer that he had been asked "what do you want?" He had replied that he wanted immediate transfer off the ship, to a shore duty station in the Pacific Northwest. And a telephone call to the USN Personnel Command had resulted in the immediate issuance of transfer orders to that duty station. The Radioman departed, bulging seabag over his shoulder, to his new shore duty assignment. SURFPAC was subsequently informed that the investigation had determined that there was no truth to the report of physical assault on a crewman by a senior officer aboard the ship. And REFTRA went on. And the passageways gleamed the next day as always. But the XO had a new nickname used behind his back by the members of the crew: "Boots."

P.S.: As you already know, the Captain DID make admiral. The XO was eventually given command of a destroyer, subsequently promoted to Captain (O-6) and assigned as a Destroyer Squadron Commander and an Aircraft Carrier Division Chief of Staff before his retirement. Such is the nature of Navy life.

CHAPTER 13

The Haircut

When I was Communications Officer of a Guided Missile Cruiser, I enjoyed the company of some excellent sailors across several ratings. None of my men were better than my Signalmen. Before their historic rating was disestablished in 2003, Signalmen specialized in visual communications, using signal flag hoists, flashing light, and semaphore. They were Morse code wizards. Visual communications are efficient and inherently secure and discreet. Unless the enemy is there, close enough to visually read the message, they cannot tell it has been sent, or what it says. Visual communications give no indication of the ship's presence or location beyond visual range. Flags don't require electricity and flashing lights can be battery-powered vice AC- powered. This can be very useful.

I always enjoyed the historic and traditional aspects of naval service. I tried to learn about them when time permitted. My Signalmen appreciated my interest and taught me what they could about their trade. I learned to read signal hoists and run a flagbag. I learned semaphore well enough to be able to read and send short messages accurately. I learned enough flashing light Morse code to recognize a hailing call, my own ship's call sign, and how to send "AS", which means "wait" – so when we received a light hail, I could tell the sender to wait...while I fetched a Signalman! I had a great relationship with these seagoing professionals.

Medium-sized ships like mine have small crews. In our case, the ship had only a very few Ship's Servicemen (now since 2019 known as "Retail Services Specialists" (pardon my eyeroll). These men specialize as barbers, laundrymen, cobblers, tailors and store clerks. And only one of these was a trained barber. Maintaining uniform regulations is a full-time responsibility, so the line at the ship's barber shop was always long, and he stayed busy. A sailor needing a haircut often had difficulty fitting it in to his off-watch time periods. So my Signalmen decided to find a better way.

One day, I walked into the signal shack high on the O-3 level aft of the bridge. The "Skivvy Wavers" (a term of endearment for Signalmen, referring to them waving underwear as semaphore flags in an emergency) were gathered around one Second Class Petty Officer holding a shiny new pair of electric barber clippers. He had bought them and brought them aboard so that the whole gang could have fresh haircuts when needed, no waiting at the ship's barber shop required. Now this kid was hilarious. An Oklahoma farm boy nicknamed "Okie" of course, he had enjoyed something of a storied local celebrity in junior rodeo back in Oklahoma. He actually had a grainy home video of himself riding a bull... and being thrown and hooked while in the air. You could actually see the cringe-worthy detail of the horn tip ripping his kneecap off, and the little bit of Okie flying across the arena. (It was retrieved and reattached, but his rodeo career was over.)

Okie was bragging about how he could cut hair, and looking for a customer. Good-natured ribbing was flying about the shack. I walked in and stopped to listen. Big mistake. Somehow, a subtle challenge was made: "Come on, Sir! You look like you could use a haircut...unless you're scared..." Etc. What could I do? So I said, "Sure! As a matter of fact, I DO need a haircut." And I sat down in the chair as Okie wrapped a bedsheet around me as a cape.

Six sets of eyes watched as Okie turned on the clippers. He made a tentative pass or two, not yet cutting, just getting his motion down, like a practice golf swing. And then, his first pass. **Bzzzzzzt.** Six sets of eyes flew open wide and bulged out....and there was a mad dash for the exit door. Every man fled the scene except Okie and me. He was definitely nervous. I could tell that the "trim" was now going to be a bit more extreme than planned. No worry, we were at sea anyway, and there is an old Navy saying: "Do you know what the difference is between a good haircut and a bad haircut? Two weeks." I said "No problem. Just even it up all over, and we're good."

I sported a high and tight buzz cut for the next few weeks. The Signal Gang took great delight in razzing both of us about it.

CHAPTER 14

The Best Detail Ever! Not.

One of the lesser-known "benefits" of sea service in the late 20th Century was the rarely-seen "Having a Beer At Sea." USN ships are dry – no alcohol is allowed on board except in two narrowly-defined cases. One: an international representational event, like a wardroom dinner party for foreign guests and officers whose services do habitually drink wine. Then, by express special permission for that one occasion, wine may be served. Two: If a ship has been at sea for over 90 consecutive days without a port visit, the command may hold a barbecue topside, also sometimes known as "steel beach." The sailors who wish to may queue up and receive two, exactly two, cans of beer. This beer must be opened and consumed right then and there, topside. There is no saving back one for later, and no transferring custody of your beer to another shipmate. None. This is carefully overseen by officers and Chief Petty Officers to ensure that the rules are strictly followed.

Flash forward a couple of years from the last deployment. My ship is preparing for a new deployment, and the supply officer realizes that he has a storeroom full of two-year old cheap beer. It has been languishing below decks all that time, unrefrigerated, and is undoubtedly no longer fit for human consumption. It must be gotten rid of, to make room for a new stock of beer to be issued if needed during the upcoming deployment. But we are talking about a thousand or more cans of beer! I am assigned as Officer in Charge of a working party detailed to this purpose. Sailors are fighting each other for the chance to volunteer for what they think is going to be a prime opportunity to steal or drink copious quantities of free beer, on duty. The Supply Officer explains that for liability reasons, we can't just dump the cases of beer off somewhere; someone might discover it, drink it, get sick from spoiled beer, and perhaps even die. No, the beer most be POURED OUT, to flow away or evaporate. No, we can't pour it into the harbor; this would be illegal marine pollution.

Eventually, we hit upon a plan. We load the beer onto a truck and drive it and the picked detail of about six sailors and me over to a beachside base recreation area at NAB Coronado. That picnic area has two large dumpsters sitting there, beautifully empty. And the sailors, solemnly briefed that no beer is to be consumed at all, begin opening cans of beer and pouring them into the dumpsters, then tossing in the empty cans. The problem is, there are over a thousand cans of beer. Pouring each one out takes time. We are going to be there all day and all tomorrow at this rate. Finally, a young seaman has an idea. Palm a can of beer, smash it onto an angle iron or other edge of the dumpster, tearing a big gash in the can, then dump quickly and toss in the can. Repeat. Repeat. Repeat......pretty much *ad infinitum*.

After several hours of work in the hot San Diego sun, we return to the ship, mission complete, and with six sober sailors pretty much soaked and reeking of stale, spoiled beer.

Their shipmates were extremely envious of them, having been selected for what they assumed was the best working party detail ever. I understand it was some time before any of the men wanted to drink a beer again.

CHAPTER 15

Don't Antagonize a Superior Officer

The Navy sets great store by the concept of seniority. Whichever line officer is senior to the other is in charge, period. No matter competence, ability, or lack thereof. Seniority is seniority, and it is closely and jealously guarded. And seniority can literally be measured in infinitesimal increments. Officers have what is called a Lineal Number. The lower the number, the more senior the officer. Two officers of the same rank may have been commissioned on the same day, but one is assigned a lower number, and is therefore eternally senior, unless the other is promoted in rank over him. The Lineal Numbers are kept in a big book, and every ship has a copy and is instantly aware of who is senior to whom. It's almost an obsession. And you don't EVER want to get on the bad side of an officer senior to you. He might just sit on your next promotion board. When in company, whichever ship's Commanding Officer is senior is automatically in charge of all the others.

Two anecdotes illustrate the point:

I. In the early 1980s, the WWII Battleship *USS NEW JERSEY* (BB-62) was extensively modified and recommissioned at Long Beach Naval Shipyard. My ship was there undergoing a year-long baseline overhaul at the same time. *NEW JERSEY* was a seagoing behemoth, bigger, heavier and of a much more storied history than any other ship in the area. Her Captain (O-6) was a hot-running future admiral, who had been given the best command assignment in decades. The Navy spared no expense or trouble to get *NEW JERSEY* back in commission. This process included having shipyard workers clock into jobs aboard us regular peons, and then disappear to go work on *NEW JERSEY*, so that she would be delivered "on time and under budget." The strategy worked, and she was. But a lot of other ships got tired of her getting top billing and the best of everything. It tends to grate on a sailor after a time.

    After she was commissioned, *NEW JERSEY* was assigned to a Surface Action Group for a little "show the flag" cruise, and she had several other ships with her as supporting players. They performed exercises and steamed about smartly, showing the flag. One of the ships assigned to this little flotilla was an aged amphibious transport ship. These unsung heroes deliver Uncle Sam's Misguided Children (USMC – the Marines) wherever they need to go to kick someone's ass as directed by higher authority. It is an unglamorous duty, as it somehow lacks the dashing esprit of a cruiser or destroyer. It certainly doesn't compare to a freshly painted and spit-shined battleship. So I can understand how NEW JERSEY's acclaim must have chafed some of the 'gator's crew.

One of the exercises ships usually perform when in company for show is called "Pass In Review", and it dates back to the age of sail. Everybody lines up, and sets a fairly slow, steady speed. The last ship in line hauls out, speeds up, and passes everyone else, rendering salutes as they pass. Whomever is junior initiates the salute when it happens – seniority is everything, remember, and juniors initiate, seniors return salutes. Then the next ship, now last, repeats the process until everyone has had their turn to pass and salute or be saluted. It's all very dignified and traditional.

So "Pass In Review" was ordered. Here came the Amphibious Transport. And just when they got alongside *NEW JERSEY* (whose Captain was senior to all), things got interesting. *NEW JERSEY's* Captain got on the bridge to bridge radio, and called the Amphib's Captain (an O-5 Commander) , saying "Commander, I don't appreciate your sentiments." When the poor junior CO professed lack of understanding, he was directed to look at his starboard quarter. There, some pissed-off junior sailor had hung a large banner made of bedsheets on the helicopter deck safety nets, painted with the immortal words "BIG J SUCKS".

A tiny figure dressed in khaki, believed to be the Amphib's CO, was seen running aft at full speed but couldn't run back there fast enough to tear it down before lots of other sailors saw it too. And so a legend was born.

Amphibious Transport

II. Friday afternoons off San Diego, California used to be a busy time. Several ships would have been at sea operating for a few days, and everyone would be returning for the weekend. Ships would start jockeying for position in a long line, as everyone can't enter port simultaneously. Ships need tugs to assist them in tying up, harbor pilots are sometimes required, and the channel can't hold everyone at the same time. So, some get to go first, and some have to wait their turn.

The line had formed one Friday afternoon, and my Captain (O-6) was on the bridge in his chair, reigning over his maritime kingdom. (This is the Screamer of Legend who has figured prominently in several earlier Sea Stories. He was usually the most senior captain in the group, and always insisted that the line be formed in order of seniority.)

The Commanding Officer (O-5) of a *SPRUANCE*-class destroyer back in the line somewhere got impatient. He had command of a fast, maneuverable, gas-turbine powered greyhound and I guess it had gone to his head. So he hauled out, rang up fast bells and began a dash for the channel entrance, figuring that he would just slip into line and no one would notice. Ahhh, no.

My skipper sat bolt upright in his chair, grabbed the bridge-to-bridge radio, and called over to the destroyer and asked to speak with the CO. "*Speaking*", came the reply. And my Captain announced, for all ships present to hear: "*That would be the worst mistake of your career, Commander.*"

A subdued "*Roger, out*" was immediately followed by a chastened destroyer slowing and resuming its place in the back of the line.

A SPRUANCE-class Destroyer

CHAPTER 16

The Great Payroll Robbery

During my tour as an Admiral's Aide and Flag Lieutenant in Norfolk, Virginia, a hilarious set of events occurred. This was 1986. Paydays aboard Navy ships were still conducted in cash, if the sailor wanted to be paid in cash. The Disbursing Officer (a junior Supply Corps officer) would be accompanied by a senior enlisted Disbursing Clerk (DK, now part of the Personnel Specialist rating, PS.) They would go to the local on-base credit union, draw large sums of cash in a leather bag, and transport it to the ship. The DK would, in good Navy fashion, draw a .45 caliber pistol from the armory, and place it unloaded into a flapped leather holster, with two 5-round magazines in a flapped magazine carrier. Presto, the cash was guarded. All secure, as far as the USN was concerned. And better yet, there was zero chance of a negligent discharge of the pistol that the Navy couldn't be bothered enough to adequately train the man with. Carry on smartly. Once payday was over, the process would be repeated in reverse, and the remaining cash returned to the credit union's vaults.

Enter the villain. A former enlisted Marine was an off-base roommate of one of the ship's junior enlisted Disbursing Clerks. And this sailor told the Marine all about the routine of cash payday. This seemed too easy a target to pass up, I guess. So late on payday (after payment had been made aboard, and while returning the residual cash,) the Disbursing Officer and Disbursing Clerk got out of a car in the parking lot of the credit union with a leather bag and a pistol belt on the DK. The former Marine approached them briskly and pulled out a Kabar combat knife, leveling it at the DK's chest and demanding that he hand over the bag. For a split second, time stood still. And then the Disbursing Officer hotfooted it into the bank, abandoning the DK at knifepoint with the bag o'money. The DK opted to do as the robber demanded, and handed over the bag, as well as the pistol belt, .45 pistol and magazines. The former Marine got into his car and peeled out of the Credit Union parking lot, running a stop sign and speeding out the Base gate, laying rubber and making tracks.

At this time, Navy bases were guarded by civilian contract security guards. One of the Base rent-a-cops saw the man run the stop sign… so he established hot pursuit to issue a traffic summons! Naturally, he called for backup, and a second base security guard joined the chase. As the Marine sped down Interstate 64, the bank robbery alarm was spread over the radio, and numerous Norfolk PD and Virginia State Troopers joined the now-serious chase. It looked like a circus with a long line of flashing lights in high-speed column. So, the Marine realized that he had to take drastic action to break the pursuit. HE BEGAN THROWING HANDFULS OF CASH OUT OF THE WINDOWS OF THE CAR. Hundreds of twenty-dollar bills floated on the afternoon breeze like cherry blossoms in May. Cars pulled over and drivers began chasing fluttering bills like butterflies in the interstate median. It was apparently quite the madhouse.

Somehow during all this, the Marine loaded the .45. He tried to pull off a last-minute swerve onto an interstate off-ramp, hoping to cause the closest cop car to overshoot, but he lost control and got stuck in the off-ramp curtilage. He leaped out of the car and ran towards the tree line. The original two civilian Base security guards (still in the lead of the procession) screeched to a tire-burning halt, and jumping out with their .38 Special revolvers drawn, ordered the man to HALT! The Marine turned towards them with the .45 extended. The Security Guards blazed away, emptying their service revolvers of all twelve available rounds..... without scoring a single hit. But the noise and muzzle flash had its desired effect, and the former Marine surrendered without further incident. He ultimately did a long stretch in federal prison.

Traffic was backed up on I-64 for hours. The local TV stations ran public service announcements informing motorists that PICTURES HAD BEEN TAKEN, AND THE AUTHORITIES WOULD BE CONTACTING ANYONE WHO DID NOT RETURN ANY RECOVERED CASH VOLUNTARILY. (I wonder how many dumbasses fell for that.)

USS STARK (FFG-31) on fire and listing

CHAPTER 17

Flashbacks

One of my shipmates is memorable, but not for a happy reason. And we were only shipmates for a relatively brief time. My Guided Missile Frigate was returning from a deployment to the Persian Gulf in May of 1987. When we were east of Pearl Harbor, we received Immediate precedence message traffic informing us that one of our sister ships which was still out there, the *USS STARK* (FFG-31) had been hit by two Exocet anti-ship missiles fired by an Iraqi aircraft. She was on fire, listing, and ultimately suffered the loss of 37 crew members killed. *STARK* was of identical construction to our ship, and had been with us in the Persian Gulf, performing identical duties. I won't go into the details and criticize *STARK's* actions or lack thereof, but she definitely contributed to her own mistaken identity engagement.

Some months later, we were undergoing Refresher Training (REFTRA) in Pearl Harbor. REFTRA is an exceptionally difficult and realistic 4-6 week period of training and inspection, overseen by a team chartered for that purpose. Efforts are made to put a ship through its paces, as realistically as possible. Drills are made very realistic; smoke generators will be blowing simulated smoke in passageways, electricity will be interrupted, members of the crew are designated as dead or injured, so that drill participants have to deal with casualties while simultaneously fighting fires, flooding, and battle damage. Sleep is hard to come by. Routine is regularly interrupted, night and day. It is a difficult time.

A new crewman reported aboard during all of this. He was a newly-promoted Second Class Damage Controlman (E-5). DCs are the Navy's damage control experts. They are trained and expected to fight fires, combat flooding, shore collapsing bulkheads and decks, improvise patches and basically fight for the ship's life under the worst of circumstances. And this man was a veteran of the *USS STARK*. He had been awarded a Bronze Star for his heroism during her battle for life after being hit by two missiles. He had worked with other members of the damage control party at first. But later, as fires raged throughout the forward part of the ship, he manned a firehose, alone, kneeling and lying on deck spraying cooling seawater on the outside of the missile magazine, preventing it from overheating and exploding. His actions may well have saved the ship.

USS STARK (FFG-31)'s battle damage

At the time, the man had been rated as an E-4 Hull Technician Third Class (HT3). HTs were damage control specialists, pipefitters and welders. (Their rating's "term of endearment" nickname among some shipmates was

"Turd Chasers", as they had to repair sewage lines, among other systems.) Right at this period, the Navy was resurrecting the old DC rating and populated it by splitting the HT rate. Some HTs became new DCs, others remained HTs. My shipmate had been crossed over to DC, given his experience actually fighting battle damage on *USS STARK*. This was decided for him, not by him. He was, in Navy parlance, "volun-told."

In addition to his Bronze Star, the Navy had asked this man what he wanted as a reward for his heroism. He replied that he wanted to attend welding school. This was a very astute move; welders make good money in civilian life, and this education would set him up for gainful employment for the rest of his life. So the Navy cut him orders to Welding School.

The problem was, DCs are not expected to weld anything – that's an HT rating function. So DC was not a source rating authorized for attendance at welding school. And when the man reported to the school, he was denied enrollment, as he was not of the proper rating. And the Navy cut him a new set of transfer orders, to my ship. Yes, to a ship of the same class as USS STARK, undergoing the most realistic battle damage simulations and intense training the Navy offers. Great idea.

A few days after he reported aboard, the ship underwent a gnarly simulated battle damage drill. Lights out, simulated smoke, screaming simulated casualties, simulated dead bodies lying about the decks, etc. And this man cracked. He was found wandering about the ship, dazed, talking to dead shipmates. He lost it. He was isolated, and Tripler Army Medical Center in Pearl Harbor sent over an ambulance for him. He was gently walked to the ambulance, and departed the ship en route to the Psychiatric Ward at Tripler. We never saw him again and forwarded his personal effects to the hospital when transfer orders detaching him from our ship were received shortly thereafter.

I've never really forgiven the USN for that particular bit of bureaucratic cruelty.

CHAPTER 18

Murder Aboard Ship

Like any other group of people, Navy sailors are a cross section of our society. And occasionally, people do horrific things to each other. It is our nature as a species, and we all would do well to remember it. Never underestimate the capacity of your fellow man for depraved violent behavior. I've always tried to live my life according to a very simple code: *"Be nice to everyone you meet. But have a backup plan to kill them if things don't go well."* These are words to live by.

I am aware of at least two documented murders which took place aboard Navy ships in the 1980s. There were a few other "suicides" by jumping overboard at night in cold waters which may or may not have actually been murders, but "dead men tell no tales" and the bodies were never recovered.

One of these murders took place aboard a *Spruance*-class destroyer. It was late evening, after a cash payday aboard the ship. The Disbursing Officer was working late in his office, balancing his accounting books and counting the leftover cash prior to returning it to the bank the next day. The Sounding and Security watch reported to the quarterdeck that they had found the Disbursing Office open, with the safe standing open and the Disbursing Officer nowhere to be found. After attempts to locate the officer failed, it began to look like he might have absconded with the money. But his car was still in the parking lot near the pier. A search of the ship discovered the officer's body, shot to death in a closed fan room in the after part of the ship. Not long after, an observant bank officer was auditing the contents of safe deposit boxes in the care of his bank, and noticed that numerous blank US Government checks were stored in one box. He called the authorities, and an investigation showed that these checks' serial numbers had been assigned to the ship in question. They had been stolen from the safe during the robbery. The holder of the safe deposit box was a petty officer assigned to the ship. He eventually admitted to having brought a personally-owned firearm aboard, and having used it to take the Disbursing Officer at gunpoint, order him into the fan room, and then to execute him there.

The other case was even more senseless. A classmate of mine was directly involved, and was best friends with the victim. His ship, an aging steam-powered Guided Missile Destroyer, was operating at sea. One of the Engineering Department's junior enlisted sailors, a young African American, was not performing well, and the Chief Engineer (who was White), as his department head, had informed him that he would not be recommended for advancement in the upcoming examination cycle. The sailor took exception to this and claimed that this was evidence of racial discrimination against him. He concealed a Kabar combat knife in his coveralls, and found the Chief Engineer in the stifling and noisy Forward Fireroom, alone in a firing alley between two operating boilers. He stabbed the officer in the chest and left him to die. The Chief Engineer was able to crawl to an escape trunk and make his way up a vertical ladder, through an escape hatch and onto the main deck of the ship. He was seen there and several sailors responded to try and save him. He bled to death on deck in my classmate's arms, but only after gasping out the name of his murderer. A subsequent search of the killer's locker found the bloody knife, wrapped in his bloodstained coveralls.

It pays to remain aware at all times.

FFG-7 Class Frigate's Gun

CHAPTER 19

Rule Two....Oops.

Most of us are familiar with the four basic rules of firearms safety:

1. Treat all weapons as always loaded.

2. Never cover anything with the muzzle that you are not prepared to destroy.

3. Keep your finger off the trigger until your front sight is on an identified threat.

4. Be sure of your target. Know what is around it. Know what is behind it.

These rules actually have some application to naval warfare as well! I am pleased to say that the events I am about to relate predated my time on the ship in question. I was not there, but saw evidence of the event after the fact.

My Oliver Hazard Perry (FFG-7) class Guided Missile Frigate was armed with a 76mm automatic dual purpose gun. It was located on the 02-Level of the superstructure, aft of the mast and just forward of the ship's engine exhaust stack, on the ship's centerline. It fired a projectile about 3 inches in diameter, and had a ready service magazine of 80 rounds, which cycled automatically. Explosive projectiles and solid inert practice projectiles were carried. This gun wasn't much in terms of power, but it could shoot down some aircraft or slower missiles, and poke a few small holes in surface targets if needed. Hey, "love the one you're with", as the song says. It wasn't a bad shipmate, but it didn't exactly strike fear into the hearts of opponents.

My ship was undergoing refresher training, and performing a gun shoot exercise. They were using BLP, or solid, non-explosive ammunition for safety purposes. Somehow, the gun jammed, and the inspectors were watching the crew try to clear the jam and return the gun to operation. The clock was ticking.

Now, normal stow position for this gun when not in use was trained directly aft (180 degrees relative) and with the barrel horizontal, parallel to the deck. In other words, pointed directly at the exhaust stack. Violating the most basic of safety procedures, that of maintaining a safe firing bearing whenever you have a gun casualty with a round in the bore, the crew somehow returned the weapon to normal stow position as they worked the problem. And in attempting to clear the jam,.......**BOOM.** They fired the chambered round.

The projectile shot right through the stack, and through an aluminum locker full of life jackets. It looked like chicken heaven had blown up, with flotation material all over the place, apparently. And one big fragment of projectile penetrated and killed the CIWS gatling gun just behind that. Ouch.

Of course, the ship had to report this casualty back to command ashore. Word got around the squadron in a flash. And when the ship pulled into port that afternoon licking its wounds, **one of our sister ships had prominently pasted a large bullseye target on their own CIWS!** (It's nice to have friends, isn't it?)

Take a look at the photo above. The gun is in the official, fleet-mandated new stow position which was ordered for all ships of this class after this incident: super-elevated above the stack so it can do no harm. And the ship forever after sported two welded-on patches on the stack: one of about 4" diameter on the forward side, and a much larger one on the aft side. I'm sure the Turkish navy wonders what they are for.

CHAPTER 20

1MC Follies

The modern warship has numerous interior communications circuits allowing contact between various parts of the ship. But the big daddy of them all is #1 Main Circuit, also known as the 1MC. This is the general announcement system, like the PA system you remember from school. It is used whenever word needs to be passed throughout the ship and over its topside areas. It is primarily controlled from the Quarterdeck when in port, and the Bridge when at sea. Whatever is said over it can be clearly heard for quite a distance.

In an earlier Sea Story: *Quarterdeck Traditions*, I described how a 1MC announcement is made when a senior officer comes aboard. When all goes well, this is crisp, professional and exact. But sailors being sailors, sometimes things go hilariously awry when a nervous or distracted man takes the mike. Two of my most memorable 1MC mishaps are as follows.

I. One lovely Key West summer day, the *PEGASUS*-class Guided Missile Hydrofoil *USS TAURUS* (PHM-3) was in port. The quarterdeck on these small ships was a tiny section of a narrow side deck. Now a ship's bell is about the closest thing to a sacred object aboard her. It is the physical symbol of the ship's history and pride and is kept immaculately shined. As our ship was small, so was the ship's bell. Ours was literally a chromed brass bell about the size of a large cantaloupe; this style bell would also be used on a mid-sized yacht. It was fitted into a dovetail mount on the bulkhead and could be removed and taken to the bridge where it lived in a matching mount for use underway. So the bell was not permanently attached to the ship.

My Commanding Officer had gone ashore for a time. Upon his return, the Officer of the Deck saw him approaching and made to perform the appropriate traditional announcement ceremony. He grabbed the bell pull and keyed the 1MC mike. I was sitting at my stateroom desk. What I should have heard was: "(*ding ding*)...*TAURUS*, arriving." What I (and everyone else in Key West harbor) actually heard was: "**(*ding clank bonk rumble rumble splash*) AW SH#@!**"

We had to bring in a diver to retrieve the bell from the bottom of the harbor. It took us a while to live that one down.

II. One of my sister ships in Key West, FL was the *USS AQUILA* (PHM-4). *AQUILA* was a fine ship, second-best in our squadron....ahem, ahem. (For the record, one of my oldest and still dearest friends was her XO, but AFTER the time period described here. He bears no responsibility for what happened....)

At the time, *AQUILA* was commanded by an officer of very short stature. He, like many height-challenged men, had a bit of a Napoleon complex going, and he could be a screamer when things didn't go his way. Of course, his crew had a nickname for him, used out of his earshot: "BooBoo", like Yogi Bear's diminutive sidekick. (He literally had difficulty seeing out over the bridge windows when docking, so he had a couple of short plywood platforms made to stand on during docking maneuvers. These were known as the "BooBoo boxes" aboard that ship.)

One day at sea, *AQUILA* suffered a flooding casualty in the aftermost compartment of the ship. Seawater coming into the space in large quantity shorted out the electricals and it was difficult to de-water the compartment, which was filled to the ship's waterline and more. She entered port with the ship significantly down by the stern and took care of the problem once pierside, but the fact that she had taken on so much water was significantly unusual and instantly visible.

The hydrofoils of PHM Squadron Two were supported by a shore-based activity called the Mobile Logistic Support Group (MLSG). The MLSG did a good deal of the repairs and maintenance on board the ships, which had very small crews due to size constraints. And sailors everywhere love to make fun of other sailors. So of course, these sailors took great delight in ribbing the *AQUILA's* crew about the deeply flooded compartment. They began to refer to the ship as the "*USS AQUARIUM*". This moniker stuck for a while.

Now, when in port, the hydrofoils had a single enlisted man stand watch as Officer of the Deck on the quarterdeck. And once an hour, he would be temporarily relieved on the quarterdeck by a junior sailor of the MLSG, so that the OOD could make a roving inspection below decks of his ship. During one of these rare periods, a very new, junior MLSG sailor was standing the quarterdeck watch on *AQUILA* while the OOD made his rounds. He had only been with the MLSG a short time, and had been hearing his shipmates refer to the "*AQUARIUM*" repeatedly. He honestly didn't know that her actual, official, dignified, quasi-sacred name was *AQUILA*. While this poor young sailor was holding the deck, down the pier came BooBoo, returning to his beloved command. So the unfortunate lad did what he had only very recently been trained to do. He grabbed the 1MC microphone, smartly rang the ship's bell twice and announced:

"(ding ding)...AQUARIUM, arriving."

BooBoo's pierside meltdown, including the throwing of his uniform hat, was apparently epic and instantly legendary.

USS GRIDLEY (CG-21) in her prime

CHAPTER 21

Snakes at Sea

One of the great challenges associated with Navy shipboard life is maintaining the appearance of the ship. Appearance matters a great deal, especially to promotion-minded Commanding Officers! In a tradition extending back across the millennia, great efforts are expended to keep the ship looking smart despite the destructive forces at play 24 hours a day. The salt-water spray corrodes everything it touches, the sun bleaches and destroys natural and synthetic materials alike. And topside areas are under the constant assault of....seagulls. These flying poop machines are the bane of Deck Divisions everywhere. Far from being the cute, picturesque accents beloved in seascape paintings, seagulls are actually nasty creatures; they are basically flying rats, but with preternaturally toxic bowels and better PR. So a constant state of war exists between sailor and seagull.

My first ship fairly bristled with radars, mounted on masts high above the deck. All of these radars had rotating antennae, which had to be maintained from time to time, so a sailor would have to go aloft and do whatever needed to be done to the antenna. To give him a place upon which to stand, sit, or lie, the Navy built metal-mesh platforms high on the mast, below each antenna. These were accessed by donning a safety harness, climbing a ladder welded to the mast, opening and passing though a trap door, then closing it to restore the safe platform.

The seagulls thought that the radar platforms made just dandy nesting, sitting and pooping sites. They loved to congregate up there in their bazillions. The decks under the radar platforms were bio-hazard zones, unless they received constant attention.

Our First Lieutenant (the officer in charge of the Deck Division, the legendary Boatswain's Mates) was desperate to try anything that might deter the daily seagull conventions. He became aware that seagulls aren't too bright....and they are, like most birds, deathly afraid of snakes. Aha! A new weapon was introduced into the everlasting war between man and seagull.

Several rubber snakes, (the kind you buy for your grandkids when their mom is terribly scared of snakes) were pressed into naval service. They were placed on the radar platforms, zip-tied in place, and ordered to maintain a 24-hour seagull watch. They stood their watches stoically, without complaint, and at all times. And they did in fact greatly reduce the pooping problem, as most of the seagulls suddenly determined that they had pressing business elsewhere when they came to alight on the platforms.

All was going so well. One day, the SPS-10 Surface Search radar antenna developed a problem requiring local maintenance. An experienced Electronics Technician was tasked to go aloft and work his "Twidget" magic. (In Navy parlance, a technical specialist is often called a "Twidget" as a term of deprecation/endearment.) The young lad had not been aboard long, as he had been recently assigned to the ship after service on another vessel. He was a city boy, urbane and sophisticated. He donned his safety harness, clipped his toolbag to his belt, and jauntily ascended the mast to perform his special brand of skill. He unfastened the trap door, swung it up, and climbed one more rung, poking his head up above platform level......and coming eye to eye with a menacing rubber rattler about six inches from the tip of his nose.

"YEEEAAAAUUUUGHHHHH"! came the ear-splitting cry from high above the deck. It sounded much like politician Howard Dean's famous (and career-ending) shriek of battle lost in the 2004 presidential election, but with overtones of sheer terror mixed in. A brief flurry of activity followed, accompanied by a stream of fluent profanity. Once his heart rate settled back down, the young ET went up on the platform, completed his mission, and returned to the relatively safe confines of the ship. He lived to tell the tale.

For the next month or so, when the ET would walk into a compartment or gaggle of shipmates topside, someone was almost certain to acknowledge his presence with a rousing "YEEEAAAAUUUUGHHHHH"! More than a few called him by his new nickname: "Snake."

He was not amused.

CHAPTER 22

The Iranian F-14

In 1985, I was deployed to the Indian Ocean aboard a Guided Missile Cruiser assigned as Air Defense Coordinator (AW) for a carrier battle group. Given that we were the boss of air defense for this powerful flotilla, we were stationed quite far from the Carrier, up the most likely threat axis for air attack: towards the Islamic Republic of Iran. It may seem strange, but we have been bitter adversaries with Iran for over 40 years, and tensions between us are nothing new. They have always been full of bluster, and have periodically issued pointed threats to attack US forces. We quite rightly take them seriously, as they are just crazy enough to try it.

In those days, Iran still had a few F-14 Tomcat fighters in their inventory, in flyable condition. Yes, that's right, the **real** star of the movie *Top Gun*, the awe-inspiring F-14. We had previously sold the Shah of Iran several, and the Mullahs had inherited his air force when they deposed him and took over. The Iranians had fitted their Tomcats with early-generation Maverick missiles: fairly crude, but guided missiles with an actual TV camera in the nose which was used to steer the weapon to its target. They could not sink a ship, but could certainly damage it and cause casualties, so they were nothing to sneeze at.

I was qualified and stood my watches as Ship's Weapons Coordinator/Force Weapons Coordinator (SWC/FWC). I was charged to determine if an air target needed to be killed, to select which weapon to use to kill it, and to issue that order to either the weapons system operator on my own ship, or to the SWC on another ship of the battle group, or to the appropriate aircraft stationed overhead to defend the force. It was an awesome responsibility for a young officer. Of course, it was intended that I would be doing this under the direction of my CO, or a more senior officer, if we had taken the ship to full battle readiness, a condition of readiness called "General Quarters."

Late at night on one midwatch, my ship picked up an air contact over the Indian Ocean. It was not operating any Identification Friend or Foe (IFF) beacon, so was utterly unidentified. It was at medium altitude, just sort of lazily bumbling around over the ocean, generally meandering towards us. Not a particular threat, but we of course took notice and tracked the contact. (AW motto: *In God We Trust; All Others We Track.*)

The midwatch is very quiet. Everybody who can be is asleep. Nothing much happens – usually. Just about the time that the contact got close enough to us to begin considering it as a possible threat, our Electronic Warfare sensor operator reported that it had energized a radar. And this radar (the AWG-9) only had one home: inside the nose of an F-14. And all our F-14's were onboard the carrier for the night.

Yeow. We had an Iranian F-14, inbound, with his targeting radar on, and no IFF signal. Call me crazy, but that looked just like the kind of threat that it was my job to stop. There was no time to wake up the Captain and ask permission. There was no aircraft available to intercept the bogey and shoo him away. So I did what I was tasked to do. I electronically and verbally issued orders to my Weapons System officer to arm two live surface-to-air missiles and place them on the launch rails, and to energize and lock two SPG-55B missile guidance radars onto the F-14. These incredibly powerful radars would have lit up the F-14's threat warning receiver like a Christmas tree.

My Weapons System Operator was a bit incredulous at first, verbally asking if I meant what I said. (Nothing like this usually happens on the midwatch, remember?) I assured him that I did indeed mean what I had ordered. I won't repeat the exact language used, as this is a family-friendly story. He got the message.

Two white birds (live missiles) zipped out of the forward missile magazine and onto the launcher. Two radars began microwaving the pilot like a frozen burrito. And with warning lights flashing and "you're about to die" beeping sounds shrieking in his headset, the Iranian pilot realized the error of his ways, extinguished his radar, and ran for home like a scared chicken.

About the time the Iranian was outbound, my Captain appeared in CIC in his undershirt, to see what all the ruckus was about. He satisfied himself that all was well, bade us put the toys away, and returned to sleep. I heard no more about the matter and life went on. But we had no more unexpected Tomcats disturbing our midwatches.

CHAPTER 23

The Loss of Sundowner 201

Naval service is inherently hazardous. Ships are complex machines with lots of moving, hot, sharp, electrically charged, explosive, radioactive or toxic things in them. And to top that off, the ocean environment will kill you given half a chance.

I remember thinking about this one night on deployment to the Western Pacific. My ship was Air Defense Coordinator for a Carrier Battle Group. One of the primary weapons the Battle Group had for its defense was two squadrons of F-14 Tomcat fighters. These planes and the men who flew in them were incredibly impressive.

They were formidable instruments of war, made even more deadly by an unheralded assistant, the Air Intercept Controller.

Air Controllers were relatively senior enlisted Operations Specialists. They were trained and tasked to assist the air crews in finding their assigned targets in the middle of an enormous sky, and getting the plane into position to kill it if necessary. A fighter aircraft's radar is contained in the nose of the plane, and it looks at a very limited cone of space in front of the aircraft. It is also limited in range and power. It just can't see very much. An Air Controller, seated aboard a ship or surveillance aircraft with a much larger radar, could see the enemy further away, and could calculate what heading and speed the fighter needed to use to make a successful intercept of the target, given its own heading and speed. The Controller would then verbally and electronically give the pilot heading and speed vectors to make intercept. Controllers were issued individual radio call signs and talked directly to the pilots. It was a close and successful partnership. (The best controller I ever knew was an E-6 Operations Specialist, issued call sign "Shogun". He was promoted to Chief Petty Officer and later went on to become an officer. I learned a great deal about a lot of things from this guy.)

One night watch, another controller on my ship was working with an F-14 from Fighter Squadron 111, the "Sundowners". Their aircraft wore distinctive tail markings of a setting sun, and used identifying nose numbers in the 200 series. This particular aircraft was Sundowner 201. All was normal, a simple, routine Combat Air Patrol (CAP) mission was going smoothly. Suddenly, the aircraft had an unrecoverable mechanical problem. The pilot declared a "mayday" emergency, indicating that loss of life was possible. The plane basically stopped flying, and the crew had to eject into the Pacific Ocean before it crashed, literally a thousand miles from land. They were over a hundred miles from the nearest ship of the battle group. The Air Controller marked the last known position of the plane, reported the mayday and our ship turned towards the site at maximum speed. The carrier launched a Search and Rescue helicopter which proceeded at best speed to the crash site.

Fortunately, everything worked out well this time. Neither of the aviators had been significantly injured on the ejection. The Pacific Ocean was relatively calm and relatively warm. The aircrew found each other in the water and joined up. And the Rescue Helicopter found them using the accurate position provided by the Air Controller. Both men were rescued and returned to the carrier safely. We were fortunate. But Mother Ocean never sleeps.

USS TAURUS (PHM-3)'s Nose Cone

CHAPTER 24

The Nose Cone

The PEGASUS-class Guided Missile Hydrofoils were unique ships, built for extreme speed and maneuverability. The ship literally flew on "cold steel wings" submerged in the water, with the hull well above the surface. Rear foils were huge wings in a shallow "W" configuration. The forward foil was an inverted T-shaped wing, with a lifting surface and a swiveling strut which acted as a canard rudder. Both were made of precipitation hardened stainless steel. The wing portion was bolted to the strut using numerous heavy and enormous steel bolts and nuts, which of course would have created significant hydrodynamic drag had they not been faired off. To make everything smooth and slippery, a cast aluminum nose cone was placed forward of the forward foil's butt joint, and fastened to the foil with four through-bolted tangs. The nose cone also contained the fathometer sensor, allowing us to determine water depth below the ship.

One night on patrol, the ship was flying along smoothly as always. There was a noise and a sudden jolt, and the ship's flight characteristics felt different. And we lost the fathometer depth reading. After a while, we determined that our normal speed of about 50 knots was drastically reduced. We watched a while longer to confirm. While still able to maintain foilborne flight, we were definitely going much slower than normal. We surmised that we had possibly flown into a drifting fishing net and were dragging it through the water. So we landed the ship and retracted the forward foil to have a look. In the dim deck lighting, we could tell that there was nothing snagged on the forward foil, so we re-extended it and took off again. Takeoff was slow and felt strange. Flight was still awkward and slow. So after a while, we landed, retracted and inspected again. And this time, we saw that the entire nose cone was missing. It had literally broken off in flight, and we were ramming the un-faired butt joint of the forward foil through the water as we flew. This was an "A-HA!" moment.

Based upon our experience, our other five sister ships immediately inspected their nose cones and found that the areas around the fasteners all showed evidence of stress and wear from years of flight. Normal landing procedure was to cut power and let the ship gradually stall into a soft landing. Our ship's CO at the time was a rash and immature LCDR (O-4) exercising the total authority of his first command without ever having been Executive Officer (second-in-command) of anything before. Think of a sixteen-year-old being given the keys to a Ferrari with a full tank of gas. He liked to do wild and unpredictable things, just for the thrill of it. And he loved to "Rapid Land" the ship – cutting the throttle and then immediately setting full foil depth. This resulted in a near-full speed nose-first dive into the sea, with a huge splash. Such fun! But it placed major stresses on the nose cone repeatedly. And ours ultimately failed.

Spare nose cones are not an inventory item, to say the least, and Boeing Aerospace's Marine Division (which had made the ships) had been disbanded. No molds remained to cast a new nose cone for us. So the ship was ordered to proceed to a small shipyard in Pensacola, FL, which had not long before completed a periodic overhaul on us. They had to special order enormously thick aluminum plate, chuck it in a huge bending press, and then machine several pieces which would fit together and replicate the shape of the original nose cone. They were able to do this in a few weeks, and we returned to service with a shiny new nose.

When we left the yard, they presented us with a small wooden plaque, with a machined scale model of a nose cone attached to it. Attached to the cone was a small stainless steel wire lanyard, locking it to the plaque "so we couldn't lose this one."

CHAPTER 25

The Sonobuoy

One of my collateral duties as a junior officer on my first ship was to be its Intelligence Officer. I was put in custody of a bunch of classified publications, and tasked to remain up to date with the tactical threat situation in the ship's area of operations, while providing a daily briefing on these matters to the Captain. I was also supposed to keep my eyes open for opportunities to submit Intelligence Information Reports (IIRs) on anything that might be of interest to the Naval Intelligence community. I was pretty busy, so this particular set of duties got relatively little of my attention.

One day in 1985, we were deployed to the Indian Ocean as part of a carrier battle group. The Russian Navy decided to come have a look at us, and sent an IL-38 "May" anti-submarine surveillance aircraft to fly and snoop around. Airplanes can and do hunt for submerged submarines. Among the tools used to do this are disposable sensors called sonobuoys. A sonobuoy is a battery-powered miniature sonar system. It is dropped into the ocean, and the upper part floats there. It then deploys a microphone on a wire deep into the water, where it either listens quietly, or transmits sound pulses and listens for return echoes. A radio system sends the information it hears back to the aircraft, which displays and uses it to try and locate the submarine, and if possible, to identify what type of boat it is. Anti-submarine aircraft carry dozens of these buoys and deploy them in search patterns.

This Russian IL-38 apparently wanted to take a peek and see if perhaps our battle group had an attack submarine supporting it, so it deployed several sonobuoys around us, and eventually flew back to its airfield. Some hours later, my ship happened to be steaming near where a fighter escort from our carrier reported that it had dropped a buoy. We diverted a little, and visually spotted the buoy! I convinced the Captain to let us recover it, so we launched a small boat and fished it back out of the water and brought it aboard. We placed it in a large barrel of fresh water to preserve it, and I took photos and sent an IIR to the Fleet Intelligence Center, Pacific (FICPAC) in Pearl Harbor. I thought that would be the end of it. But FICPAC got excited! They had previously recovered old, badly corroded examples of this type of buoy, but never one that was still in fresh, operable condition. They sent an enlisted Intelligence Specialist from the carrier over to us by helicopter, and he took the buoy back with him. It was flown back to Pearl, and I gather it was dissected to determine its construction and likely capabilities. My ship got a nice "attaboy" commendation for providing it. Sometimes even floating trash is valuable.

CHAPTER 26

The Supply System, or Larceny As A Way Of Life

One of the aspects of my naval service which I never understood was the pervasive acceptance of the notion that if you needed something, it was okay to steal it from someone else rather than getting the Navy supply system to do its job and get it for you. Many senior leaders actively encouraged subordinates to do whatever they had to do, and to steal whatever they needed to steal for short-term gain, apparently mindless of the negative effect this had on both the system and the victims of theft. This was closely associated with the under-reporting of broken or inoperable equipment, based on the theory that if your ship's capability was degraded by a broken system, you were somehow at fault and less successful in your command. This supposedly made you less competitive for promotion than your peers.

The Navy had a system of Casualty Reports (CASREPs) which was intended to let the Chain of Command know the exact status of material readiness of your ship at any time. It is impossible for any ship to be 100% perfect at any time; there will always be some system degraded or inoperative at any given moment. Ships are incredibly complex machines. So when a major system was degraded or inoperable, you were supposed to send a CASREP to let the chain of command know. They could then make good decisions based upon your ACTUAL combat readiness, vice your cosmetic or apparent state of readiness. Perhaps they could apply pressure to get you the part or assistance you needed to fix the issue. But many CO's were hesitant to send CASREPS, as they also had another effect; they invited senior leadership's attention to your ship's problem. Leadership required that you actually take action to fix it, while keeping them informed. And apparently, "the part is on order" wasn't a good enough answer to deflect this unwanted higher command attention. Rather than making the Supply System respond in a rapid, responsive manner, they allowed it to drag its feet and to practice mediocrity in function, by circumventing it. To my way of thinking, this was counterproductive. Better by far would be to have the Chain of Command know your ACTUAL state of readiness, and apply whatever pressure was needed to make the Supply System do its job.

A few examples of the "Larceny As A Way Of Life" culture I experienced:

I. When I reported to my ballistic missile submarine for my 3rd Class Midshipman cruise, the boat was at sea for sea trials prior to departing on patrol. The only crew's officer ashore was the junior Supply Officer, a Supply Corps ensign. I was assigned to accompany him as he did the last-minute things needed to get the boat underway on schedule, with all needed supplies aboard. He took me with him as he visited a large supply warehouse to retrieve ordered parts and supplies which had been recently delivered. The warehouse supported several different submarines, and each boat had a large fenced-off cage with a locked gate, to segregate items ordered by and belonging to them. The Baby Chop (Supply Officers were affectionately called "Pork Chops", shortened to "Chop" as a nickname, as their collar insignia identifying them as a Supply Corps officer vaguely resembled a pork chop) had a clipboard with him, listing all the things which were on order but not yet delivered. He went through our mostly empty cage, looking for the items which he had dutifully color coded by priority. Lots of things were still missing. He then walked over to the cage belonging to another boat, which was at sea on patrol at the time. Their cage was full of boxes of parts and supplies which had been delivered while they were away. He whipped out a pair of bolt cutters, cut the padlock off, and went through the cage, selecting items which he determined our boat needed. I'm sure my eyes bugged out, watching him commit grand larceny. By the time he was done, many thousands of dollars of government material ordered by, delivered to, and presumably needed by another fleet unit had found a new home in our cage, and ultimately, aboard our boat. The rightful owners would just have to reorder and wait for delayed delivery when they discovered the loss. And the Supply System was not held accountable for not getting the stuff we needed delivered to us on time to support a ballistic missile deterrent patrol. I don't think this was the most desirable outcome.

II. As we were conducting an annual inventory of controlled equipage one day aboard my Guided Missile Frigate, my leading signalman came to me with an admission. We were missing a spyglass. Yes, an optical spyglass, used only for quarterdeck ceremonies these days, but very much a required inventory item. And as Operations Officer, I was responsible for it. The SM explained that one of his junior signalmen had lent the spyglass to another ship's signal gang, when they came aboard and asked to borrow one, as they were being inspected and didn't have theirs to show. This young SM had at least had the sense to get a hand receipt for the spyglass signed, and the borrower took the spyglass back for inspection. The problem was, after the inspection was over, they didn't return it. They DEPLOYED TO THE WESTERN PACIFIC WITH IT. I was not amused. One day a couple of months later, we made port in Pearl Harbor, and there across the harbor was the offending ship. I made my leading signalman call over on flashing light to that ship, asking to speak to the Operations Officer by flashing light. (This is unusual.). A few minutes later, intrigued, he was standing by at their light. I then explained by Morse message that I wanted my spyglass back immediately, and that I had a signed hand receipt with the serial number and name of the borrower shown on it. A brief flurry of activity later, a profuse apology replied, and my spyglass was returned by the shamefaced SM who had "borrowed" it later that afternoon. I had only had to travel 4200 miles one-way from San Diego to get it back.

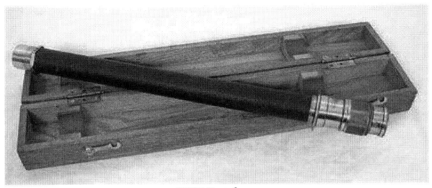

USN Spyglass

III. My first CO, the legendary Screamer, loved to tell junior officers that he expected them to be resourceful and to do whatever they had to do to achieve his desired degree of perfection. He regaled us repeatedly with the tale of one of his greatest triumphs as an object lesson. He had been Gunnery Officer aboard an ancient Destroyer Escort. His class of ship had a twin 3"x50 caliber gun mount on the forecastle. This type of gun had a large counter-recoil spring around the breech area of each gun barrel. One of his springs was cracked, making that gun inoperable, as it was unsafe to fire. No replacement was immediately available in the local supply center. The ship was moored in a nest of ships of the same class, with identical armament. So the Captain had his Gunners Mates sneak over the lifelines

3"/50 Gun Mount

on the midwatch, quietly disassemble the gun on the outboard sister ship, and swap their sound spring with his broken one. Problem solved. It's fortunate that no one got shot as an intruder.

IV. My Operations Officer on that first ship was a disciple of the Screamer CO. He agreed with the abusive leadership style, and practiced it himself. He loved to tell his own tale of supply system derring-do. As First Lieutenant (Deck Division Officer) of a destroyer home-ported in Pearl Harbor, HI, he had **run out of haze gray paint** (which is the color of paint that the entire hull and superstructure is painted with. It is a daily use item. This is an unpardonable sin, on most ships.) It would take some time to order a new stock, and he would have to admit that he had neglected to keep the proper inventory. His solution? He wandered over to the Pearl Harbor Naval Shipyard late one night, stole a forklift, and used it to steal an entire pallet of haze gray paint which was staged to paint a newly-sandblasted ship in drydock the following day. Somehow, the phrase "conduct unbecoming of an officer and a gentleman" comes to mind.

RGM-84 HARPOON Anti-ship Missile

CHAPTER 27

The Duel

In 1987, I was Operations Officer and Navigator of a guided missile frigate returning home to San Diego, CA from a deployment to the Persian Gulf. We were in company with a Knox-class frigate, and as our Captain was senior to the frigate's commanding officer, we were in tactical command. Both of our ships were armed with the Harpoon anti-ship guided missile. Now, my various ships across my naval career were armed with a variety of weapons, but the Harpoon was common to them all and was my hands-down favorite. A sea-skimming, internal radar-guided ship killer, the Harpoon packed an almost 500 pound high explosive warhead, which was delivered at speeds of over 500 mph, at targets up to 70 miles away, skimming the surface of the sea as it flew to make it difficult to detect visually or by radar. Early versions performed a steep "pop-up" climb in terminal phase, before pitching down and diving on the target at a steep angle. Later versions omitted this maneuver, (which actually made it easier to hit with a close-in defensive weapons system than simply running in at increasingly low altitude to impact.) The weapon had a couple of different modes for use. It could be fired straight at the enemy or set to fly off axis and then turn in to approach from a different bearing, so that a single ship could deliver several missiles arriving nearly simultaneously from multiple directions. If you knew pretty exactly where the enemy was, it could be targeted to a specific locational "box" in the ocean to look for its target. If you had less of an idea, you could just fire it along a likely bearing and turn its radar on and later off, to cover a larger swath of ocean while searching for its target. The operator would program the missile in whatever way the situation called for, then launch it and move on to other business, as it was a "fire and forget" missile, obtaining its own terminal guidance with its onboard radar. The Harpoon was a flexible, deadly weapon and I enjoyed learning to use it to its fullest capability as a form of maritime martial art.

As our little two-frigate surface action group was headed east across the Pacific, a matching pair of ships of the same classes was transiting west to begin their deployments. The Navy, in a rare burst of focus on combat capability rather than political correctness, ordered us to conduct a tactical exercise as we passed in mid-ocean. We were all directed to a generous sized locational box, and directed to pass through the box at the same time, with each group hunting the other and trying to sink the opponents with simulated weapons fire. This was an evenly-matched duel of ships configured with exactly the same capabilities, so either luck or superior tactics would determine the outcome. I was assigned as Tactical Action Officer for the period of the exercise, in essence fighting my ship while directing the actions of our junior partner. And I planned to win this duel.

Now, radar is a wonderful tool enabling you to "see" well beyond the horizon and in all weather and lighting, but it has one major drawback. Radar impulses can be "seen" and tracked far beyond the range at which they can detect targets. So driving around blasting radar signals into the air makes you very easy to detect and track. It is a bit like hunting an armed opponent in a dark warehouse. You don't want to go walking around shining your flashlight. It was therefore assumed that all the ships in this exercise would have all their radars turned off. All four of the ships were designed to hunt submarines, so they were all very quiet acoustically as ships go; it would be hard to hear each other using sonar. What did that mean to me? The most likely way we would detect each other would be visually – unless someone lit off a radar and tried to take a snap shot, hoping to destroy a slower enemy who was less prepared to fire back in return but who just happened to be in range. This was a risky strategy at best, as the radar signal would give all the other ships in the game an instant ability to locate the shooter. So the smart money was on a visual detection. As is so often the case in warfare, whoever saw their opponent first was likely to win.

There is a pretty simple maxim at play here. You can see farther when you are higher in the air, looking over the horizon and beyond the curvature of the earth. That is why sailing men-of-war had crow's nests and fighting tops. Modern Navy ships are bristling with high-powered radars and powerful communications antennae, the radiations from which can physically fry a human body. It is dangerous to be aloft among these systems, so normally, no one is placed high on the mast. But as we were planning to be electronically silent, and as it was a fairly calm, pleasant day in mid-ocean, I asked the Captain for permission to put a lookout on the topmost radar platform, outfitted with a safety harness, a pair of binoculars and a sound-powered telephone connecting him directly to the bridge. This greatly increased our visual detection range. We mathematically worked out what would be the approximate range of a ship whose topmasts were visible from that known height above the water. And we knew exactly how tall those masts were, as they were just like our own!

Some hours into the exercise, along the expected bearing of our opponents' approach, the mainmast lookout reported first one, then another set of masts. He relayed the relative bearings and coloration/configuration details. This was definitely our prey. We plugged the known bearing and estimated range information into our Harpoon control console, and simulated launching Harpoons at both of our opponents, using off-axis attack vectors. We then called the launch, salvo size, target geographic positions and estimated impact time out over a dedicated exercise radio circuit, thereby registering our attack. We had ordered our junior companion ship to be ready to fire should the first salvo not get the job done, after passing the details to them via visual communications (flashing light using Morse code.) We had the lookout descend quickly, and once he was on deck, lit off a surface search radar to confirm the targets; our locations were near-exact and there were no other ships in the vicinity to act as unintended targets.

No second salvo was necessary. Good guys 2, bad guys 0. Sometimes the old ways are best. Thus ended the duel.

USS MAHLON S. TISDALE (FFG-27)

CHAPTER 28

The Knife Fight

There is an unfortunate but imperative dictum which runs throughout all human life, but especially military service: LIFE ISN'T FAIR. Sometimes the conditions are stacked against you, but duty demands that you must carry on and continue your mission. This can easily get you killed, but such is the nature of warfare. And sometimes, you can win against overwhelming odds, if your spirit is up to the fight.

The *Oliver Hazard Perry* (FFG-7) class Guided Missile Frigates were outstanding little ships, but they were designed to be fairly inexpensive. The "Flight I" early versions were given modest capabilities, and optimized for operations in relatively shallow, littoral waters. They were designed to hunt submarines and were acoustically very quiet and hard to detect with passive sonar. But they had a fairly low powered, higher frequency hull mounted sonar (sometimes derisively called the "Helen Keller system"), and they embarked a practically antique helicopter, the SH-2 Sea Sprite. Later versions got better helicopters and a vastly improved towed array passive sonar, making them far more formidable anti-submarine platforms. But my ship was one of the early "Flight I" ships.

In 1988, we were undergoing Refresher Training in Pearl Harbor, HI. As part of that training period, we were ordered to participate in a combat simulation exercise against a *Los Angeles*-class fast attack submarine. Any surface ship is at a disadvantage against a submarine. The environment and odds highly favor the sub. It's a much better deal to send a helicopter out to kill him! A modern attack submarine is one of the most lethal weapons ever designed by man, and at that time, the *Los Angeles* boats were the top of the line. Quiet, fast, deep-diving and supremely deadly, an *LA* was a surface ship's worst nightmare as an opponent. My little frigate was severely over-matched. And we had no helicopter, so it was all up to us.

We were directed to proceed to a specified box in the Pacific Ocean, and there to attempt to find the submarine. Their mission was to sneak past us. This simulated the submarine passing through a guarded geographic choke point or other constrained area to engage on a further mission, something boats like this do from time to time. Recognizing that our ship's sensors were not capable of deep-water detection, the submarine was given a "hard deck" depth limitation, below which he was not allowed to operate. This simulated a shallow water littoral location instead of the deep Pacific where we actually were. Rather than a long-range engagement, this was to be an old-style knife fight between a ship and a submarine. The sub usually wins these affairs.

The exercise window began. We did our thing, quietly patrolling the box and looking for any indication of our opponent's presence. As we commenced, one of the REFTRA inspectors casually mentioned that the boat we were hunting was considered to be one of the best in the fleet, and that the Commanding Officer was a favorite or protégé of the Commander of Submarines, Pacific Fleet (COMSUBPAC). And the Admiral was personally onboard the boat. Right now.

Needless to say, the stakes of this particular game just got higher. Reputation was at stake. We had a basic idea of what the boat was perhaps likely to do. We had our mission orders. And we got a very slight trace of a contact indicating that there might be a submarine out there on a specific bearing. When you are over-matched, it is often a good idea to take the initiative. So we did! We quit trying to be quiet, brought the ship up to full speed, and making an educated guess about where the submarine was likely located, we went active on our sonar, blasting sound pulses out into the ocean and listening for echoes, like something out of World War II. And there was the boat. We nailed it.

We quickly got right over the top of the boat, and stayed there, shaking it like a terrier shakes a rat. 30+ knots of speed, hard rudder turns, the ship heeling and shuddering as the submarine beneath us tried everything possible to shake us off. He tried turning, crash stopping, firing decoys, and any other tricks in his bag, to no avail. We were later told that COMSUBPAC got increasingly irate as his boat could not break contact with a measly little Flight I FFG. Finally, after a very extended period of active contact, the Admiral removed the exercise hard deck limitation and allowed the submarine to submerge deeply below the ocean temperature thermocline, which acts as a sonic barrier. The boat slunk into the depths and was heard no more. In that environment, he would surely have evaded or destroyed us easily. But in the shallow water which we were designed for, we gave him as much as he could handle and more.

A LOS ANGELES-class SSN

In time of war, if ordered, a little ship like mine would follow her orders to take on an attack sub, no matter what. We would likely be sunk as a result. Life isn't fair. But in time of war, an attack submarine would also follow orders to try and sneak past a guard frigate in shallow water. And he might lose that knife fight, too. Life isn't fair. Sometimes the underdog wins. That was a good lesson for both of the fighters on this day.

CHAPTER 29
Cold Steel Wings

The *PEGASUS* class Guided Missile Hydrofoils were outstanding little ships, faster than any other warships and heavily armed with Harpoon anti-ship guided missiles and a rapid-fire 76mm automatic gun. Crewed by only five officers and nineteen enlisted men, they were very well-suited to littoral and choke point operations. They could linger on patrol for about two weeks hullborne, keeping a presence in key areas of interest, including shallow littoral waters. They could then be replenished at sea from a variety of support vessels, including non-traditional sources such as other line warships, and even a US Coast Guard (USCG) aerostat vessel (we did it repeatedly). When needed, they could rapidly go foilborne, flying fast on their "cold steel wings" in excess of 50 knots with extreme maneuverability, and send forth a storm of as many as eight advanced Harpoon anti-ship missiles. The entire squadron of six ships was deployable anywhere in the world, as was the shore-based Mobile Logistic Support Group which sustained them. Anywhere with a big runway or harbor which would allow bulk resupply of fuel, weapons, parts and stores could base the squadron. (Two of the ships once deployed for an extended period and successfully operated out of Georgetown, Grenada as a proof of concept. Web search "Georgetown." That is indeed proof.) This was a very potent weapon which could be risked much more cheaply and readily than a $1.8 billion dollar guided missile destroyer with a crew of 320 men. It was the modern equivalent of a WWII PT Boat, although exponentially more capable and deadly. It was built to fight.

Of course the "major combatant"-centric Navy never could get its head around how to operate these unconventional ships properly, and how to appreciate what value they provided. "They can't deploy as part of an aircraft carrier battle group, so what good are they?" asked the brass. So, they were based in Key West, Florida, and relegated to a minor backwater of late 20th century naval strategy. And they were decommissioned quite young, far before their time.

One mission the hydrofoils often were tasked with was supporting USCG counter-drug operations. To stay within the *posse comitatus* act restrictions, each ship would embark a USCG law enforcement detachment which would perform the boarding, search, seizure and arrest functions. The ship would get them to the target, feed and house them (albeit under very spartan conditions, given our very small size. LEDETs usually slept on the deck in the magazine under the gun mount forward.) We would cover them with firepower and overwatch as they did their job of search and seizure. And occasionally, we would participate as part of a larger combined operation.

In November of 1989, two hydrofoils including my ship were assigned in support of a major joint counter-drug operation which included the DEA, US Customs Service, US Coast Guard and US Navy. A small flotilla of ships, fast boats and aircraft were on patrol off the Cay Sal Bank in the Bahamas. The DEA had reason to believe that a major cocaine transshipment was about to take place, and it was our job to stop it. It was rainy, completely overcast, but with only slight seas of about 2 feet and a warm, humid air temperature. The task group was patrolling with lights out on the dark sea. An air search radar contact looked promising. And it did in fact descend below the cloud cover. Then we could see little sparks of light as large waterproofed bundles of cocaine were dropped from the aircraft into the sea with chemlights attached to each one, to be retrieved by several fast ocean speedboats waiting below for that purpose. When the bundle drop was completed and the speedboats had recovered most of the bales, the mission commander gave the order to "light 'em up!" We went foilborne, and began to chase the speedboats, as the rest of the task group maneuvered to surround the targets and retrieve the cocaine. And on this night, in these conditions, those speedboats were not going to evade a Navy hydrofoil. They were simply outmatched.

A high-speed pursuit ensued. A US Customs Service Blackhawk helicopter was right above one speeding boat, shining a spotlight right down onto it and pursuing it relentlessly. The boats, realizing that they were surrounded, began to jettison the bales of cocaine to lighten their loads and remove evidence. My ship was flying past a line of chemlighted bales, closing on our target. The helicopter chased the one speedboat relentlessly, like a terrier on a rat. And then, our sister ship's lookout reported that he had lost visual contact with the helicopter, and that it appeared that it had crashed into the sea.

Efforts to contact the helo were unsuccessful, and it became apparent that it was no longer in the air. My ship was closest to its last known position. We were told to break off pursuit and get to the crash site to rescue survivors, which we instantly did. In short order, we arrived at the location and landed the ship. Out lookouts noted debris in the water and a smell of aviation fuel. We were on site. And then we spotted several strobe lights in the water nearby. We recovered five of the six crewmembers from the helo eleven minutes after they crashed. These survivors comprised three USCS personnel and two Bahamian Customs Service policemen, who had been aboard as observers. The co-pilot was still unaccounted for, and the pilot said he thought he had felt him egressing from the sinking aircraft and that he might have heard him yell out in the darkness as the aircrew struggled to come together in the water. We extended medical treatment to the men immediately.

As a man was still missing, this now became a Search and Rescue (SAR) mission, and as the first vessel on scene, according to USCG protocols, our ship was SAR mission commander. We established a search grid, directed all available ships, boats and aircraft to assigned positions, and began an intensive search of the sea surface looking for the missing crewman. We capably directed that search effort for the next 18 hours as SAR Commander. Also during that period, we took aboard all the recovered cocaine from the smaller speedboats and other vessels which had recovered it from the ocean. In total we took custody of over 2000 lbs of pure, uncut cocaine, with a street value of millions of dollars.

As the search wore on, the pilot of the helicopter began to exhibit signs of stress and our medical crewman (actually our ship's cook, but cross-trained as an EMT) was concerned that he might be having or might have a heart attack. We were ordered to pass SAR Commander duties to the senior USCG vessel on scene and return to Key West with the survivors and the drugs. We detached from the task group and returned to port. The search continued for several days, but the co-pilot was not found alive.

His body was later discovered in the wreckage by divers, still strapped in his seat. He was the first fatality in the USCS's flight division's history.

For our actions on the night of November 02-03 of 1989, my ship was awarded the US Coast Guard Meritorious Unit Commendation, a distinction rarely extended to US Navy ships. We flew it proudly for the remainder of the ship's life in commission.

CHAPTER 30

Tight Spaces

Naval service occasionally required me to get into and out of a few tight spots. I'm not talking about potentially dangerous situations. I'm referring to actual confined spaces. Whilst traveling along life's highway, I have discovered that I'm mildly claustrophobic and mildly acrophobic. I don't like tight spaces, and I don't particularly like heights. But I have always felt that succumbing to fear rather than facing it lets that fear rule over you and limit you. So I have always tried to make myself do the things I feared. Heights? I learned rappelling, then taught rappelling, and ultimately took up parachuting. I agreed to go up on high places when a task required it, rather than begging off and making someone else go up there.

The Navy also asked me to go into some very tight, confining spaces. I am currently 6'1" tall and weigh 205 lbs. In those days I was the same height but weighed between 180 and 190 lbs. I'm not a small guy and I don't fit well into tiny places. This was therefore occasionally very uncomfortable. I clearly remember the worst of these experiences.

I.   One one midshipman cruise, I was being given a tour of a minesweeper. These tiny ships were old even then, and made of wood to reduce their magnetic signature. As many of the things aboard as possible were anti-magnetic. The tour led down a very small, round hatch in the afterdeck, and down a wooden ladder into After Steering, the rearmost compartment on the ship, which contained the steering gear. It was saturated with decades' worth of hydraulic fluid, and a bit slippery. The deck hatch (called a scuttle in Navy parlance) was about 20 or so inches in diameter. It was a very tight fit requiring me to scrunch up my shoulders to get through it. I could not see past it down into the small compartment, so was descending blind. As I was focusing on this, my foot slipped off the lowest rung, and I dropped about a foot unexpectedly. A wooden workbench was fitted into this tiny space, as there was absolutely no spare room on such a small ship, and this was a place where a work surface could be fitted. A corner of this workbench protruded directly under the ladder. I fell onto this corner, which neatly bisected my buttcrack, and I took my full weight onto my coccyx, probably cracking or breaking it. It was excruciating and I was conscious of pain there for at least the next month. I still have some pain there occasionally. Strike One for tight spaces.

II. On my Ballistic Missile Submarine, tight spaces were common, as you might imagine. My bunk, for example. It was barely wider than my shoulders, maybe a couple of inches extra on each side. Lie flat on your bed. Place your elbow into your hipbone and point your fingers towards the ceiling. Your fingertips would be touching the bottom of the bunk above you. No worries, I carried on smartly, studying and learning as much about the boat as possible. For a time I was spending my watches in the Torpedo Room, which on that class of boat was all the way forward in the nose. I learned about the torpedoes, the tubes, and their support systems which allowed it all to work. One of those clever systems was a mechanical interlock which prevents both the outer door and inner door of the torpedo tube from being open at the same time, thereby flooding and sinking the boat. (This seemed a wonderfully prudent design to me!) Torpedo tubes are also quite small: about 21 inches in diameter and about 22 or so feet in length. Take out your tape measure and look at 21 inches. The torpedo fits very tightly in the tube. There isn't any spare room for any debris or material in there. It could jam the weapon in the tube. So after every flooding of the tube with seawater, the tube is pumped empty, and some sailor actually has to crawl in headfirst and wipe it down with a rag, removing any sea life or debris which may have entered. On one watch, we actually fired a blank shot, called a "water slug" out of an empty tube to test the firing systems. I was given the honor of pushing the button. WHAM. Big jolt, big rush of compressed air. I was Clark Gable in a WWII movie. What fun. Then the leading torpedoman said "whoever fires the tube, dives the tube. That's the rule." So I was handed a rag, the tube was pumped down and the breech door opened, and I was shoved headfirst into the 21-inch tube and bade to hunch my way all the way out to the far end. This, while the boat was hundreds of feet below the surface, at patrol depth. I hunched. I wiped. I kept calm and carried on. The tube was as black as night and very cold. The Torpedo Gang was yelling "encouragements" up the tube, and directing me to kiss the muzzle door, as this was my first tube ride, and that it was "tradition." I delivered a big old smacker to the cold, wet steel door…… and they slammed the breech door shut 22 feet behind me with a resounding clang. I instantly recalled that the mechanical interlock was now bypassed, and it was at least theoretically possible that a stray electrical impulse could open the outer door to the pressure of the sea. I was not best pleased. On this class of boat, the passive sonar array was located conformally around the nose, and around the tubes. This was the boats "ears", and the means by which potential adversaries would be detected. I was later told that the Sonar Shack called down to the Torpedo Room and insisted that whoever was in the torpedo tube be let out immediately....they couldn't hear a damn thing for all the yelling that was going on. Strike Two.

III. When a ship undergoes a baseline overhaul, as much as possible is done to repair and maintain it to like new condition. This includes the sandblasting, cleaning, repriming and repainting of tank interiors. Fuel tanks on a warship are usually located in the hollow space between the outer hull and an inner hull, between adjacent structural ribs. They conform to the shape of the ship, and are mostly well below the waterline so as to keep the weight very low for stability. As having many thousands of gallons of fuel freely sloshing back and forth would be very bad for stability as well, the tanks are baffled. This means that they are subdivided with internal barriers into little cells, about the size of long coffins. There are oval scuttles connecting each cell with the adjacent ones, so fuel can drain back and forth, but it is slowed down to prevent that sloshing. One such main fuel tank on my ship had been overhauled, and was about to be bolted shut for several years. Procedure required that someone go down in the tank to make sure that all blasting grit, painting materials, stray wrenches or tools, rags or anything else which could clog the fuel system had been removed before the tank could be certified ready for service. I happened by at just the wrong moment, and was asked if I was willing to do the job. Several sets of enlisted men's eyes looked at me, wanting to see if I would demur and make some one of them do something I was not willing to do myself. To hell with that. So I said I would! I was dressed in a set of dirty coveralls and handed one of those angle-headed OD green flashlights like troops used in Vietnam. As I recall,

I went in feet first. The tank reeked of decades' worth of fuel oil which had seeped deep into the metal, even after cleaning. Hunch forward, pass through a scuttle into the next cell, then the next. Then twist and proceed through a horizontal scuttle down a level, through three or four more cells, passing through a tight scuttle each time. Then twist and down again. I was hanging in there. I got to the very end, completing my inspection, and for some dumb reason, decided to turn off my flashlight momentarily. Bad, bad mistake. If I hadn't been claustrophobic before then, I dang sure was now. It was awful, like a crushing weight rushing in on me. I knew I was far below the waterline, with all those cells to traverse before getting back to light and fresh air. I could not get that light on and get out of there soon enough. It makes the hair stand up on the back of my neck even now and I'm not sure I could do it again if I had to. It is a job for a very small and very brave man.

In case you are wondering, I have left instructions in my will that when I die, my body is to be cremated. There ain't no way I'm going back into a box that size to spend years or centuries awaiting the Resurrection. Not a chance.

CHAPTER 31

Walking Across the Pacific

In June of 1988, my Guided Missile Frigate was just completing refresher training in Pearl Harbor, HI. This had been a period of intense operational activity, with considerable stress, lost sleep and tiring evolutions. All hands aboard were looking forward to returning to our home port of San Diego, CA and to our families. A few relaxing days at sea, a nice fast transit and a couple of sea details were all that stood between us and home, sweet home. A couple of days before departure, the Captain called me into his cabin and told me (as the ship's Navigator) to prepare a navigation plan to take the ship from Pear Harbor to...

Bremerton, Washington. Unexpected tasking had reared its ugly head. This was not particularly welcome news to me, or to anyone else aboard.

One of the USN's very first class of nuclear-powered submarines, the USS SARGO (SSN-583) had recently been decommissioned at Pearl Harbor and had immediately been stricken from the naval register. Commissioned 30 years earlier in Mare Island, CA (two years before I had been born!), the old girl had served with honor through the hottest years of the Cold War. Even so, time, modern design and nuclear engineering had long since passed her by, and she was technically obsolete and fully deserving of retirement. She was to be scrapped at Naval Shipyard Bremerton. No longer crewed, her reactors cold forever, and with many vital systems totally inoperative, she could not travel there under her own power. She was to be ignominiously towed to her final resting place.

This was a job for a professional towing vessel, and the recovery and salvage ship USS RECLAIMER (ARS-42) was assigned the duty. This was very much right up their professional alley. The fly in the ointment was this: the USN was worried that some of the myriad "NO NUKES!" pinhead protesters around the world would try to take the opportunity to create an incident involving one of the world's very first nuclear-powered vessels. If they could get near her, splash some red paint on her, show a few protest signs, or even worse, manage to cut the towline and set her adrift, or board and commandeer her as a floating protest venue, they could get global press attention to their cause. Never mind that this could risk innocent lives, or cause environmental damage; the kind of idiots who perform these types of protests aren't long on brains or logic. It's all about the emotion of things. The Navy therefore decided that an escort vessel should accompany the tow all the way across the eastern Pacific, to guard against any attempts to interfere with her. And the duty fell to lucky us. We were assigned to ride shotgun over the tow mission. Should any pinheads appear, it was our job to shoo them away. We had to keep the tow in visual sight at all times.

Now, for centuries, small fast ships like frigates and destroyers have been where the excitement can be found. They are flexible, speedy, powerful and maneuverable, and small enough and cheap enough to risk doing something when a larger, more expensive ship should not be. All Navy ships perform valuable service, but frigates and destroyers are by nature exciting and busy. Serving aboard one is kind of like dating a really attractive, high-spirited woman: you get used to a certain degree of "energy" in operations. Dashing about, shootin' at stuff, ridin' like the wind, etc. breeds a certain kind of sailor. I was proud to be that kind.

The day of departure came. We waited off the Pearl Harbor sea buoy, and out came RECLAIMER towing SARGO. As senior ship, we took operational command and turned to set our course towards Bremerton. And off we went. Now, you may not realize this, but towing a 2800-ton dead weight at the end of a long nylon towing hawser is an operation harnessing tremendous forces. These must be managed and kept under control, lest damage occur or injury result from a parted tow rig. Weather and sea state affect handling and force as well. So towing is a slooooowwwww business. Instead of the dignified canter or speedy gallop we frigate sailors were accustomed to, the towing ship set a prudent speed of about 4-5 knots. That is just about a speedy walk over level ground.

For the next several weeks, we crossed the Pacific.....at a brisk walk. Ugh. Talk about boring. Think of the longest road trip in heavy traffic you have ever made, with 200 horny and homesick "kids" in the back seat asking "are we THERE yet?" ...and it going on and on and on... for weeks. It was awful. We did anything to break the boredom: dashing ahead, drifting back and letting the tow pass us, dreaming up radio and signals drills to involve the crew of RECLAIMER (who were not accustomed to having to do such, as they usually operated alone on their types of missions.

USS RECLAIMER (ARS-42)

This was as much punishment for them as lollygagging across the ocean was for us. So of course we demanded that they participate.) And not a single pinhead protester was ever sighted. We almost wished they would come, before it was over. Finally, we arrived at Bremerton, handed the tow over to the local Coast Guard patrols, and set course for home. I'm pretty sure no sailor from either of the two ships planned to send Christmas cards to each other at holiday time. Adios, shipmates. See ya. We're outta here. Hi-yo Silver, away.

Smith & Wesson .38 Revolver

CHAPTER 32

Shots Fired!

In the summer of 1990, I was finishing up my tour as Executive Officer of *USS TAURUS* (PHM-3) and getting ready to leave active duty Navy service. It was the 4th of July weekend. I had but days to go before being relieved and departing the ship and the active duty Navy.

One of the sailors onboard *TAURUS* had been experiencing some difficulty. He was an E-5 Gas Turbine Systems engineer (GSM2). This young sailor was one of only two African Americans aboard the ship, and was by nature a quiet, solitary young man. He pretty much kept to himself and had little to say outside his duties. Unfortunately, he was finding it difficult to master his rating specialty's fairly significant technical demands, and he was struggling to qualify as an Engineering Officer of the Watch (EOOW), the individual who actively monitored and controlled the main propulsion and auxiliary engineering plants. His Leading Chief Petty Officer and other division mates had tried to assist him in learning what he needed to learn, but he was just not getting it. He grew even more withdrawn as a result.

On that Saturday morning, I went to the local base firing range with a couple of the other members of the crew who were, like me, avid shooting enthusiasts. We had fun blasting away at targets for an hour or two and returned to our billets. I dropped off my shooting kit and went back into Key West for a few things my family needed. Before I returned home, my wife received a telephone call from one of the shooters, telling her "Ma'am, I need to speak to the XO RIGHT NOW!" She informed my shipmate that I was not home, and he asked her to relay a message to me as soon as possible: "Shots are being fired at the Base Enlisted Quarters (BEQ.) And please tell him it's (name of the young GSM2.)" I returned home not long thereafter, and got involved in the last kerfluffle of my active duty career.

What had happened was this. A few sailors had pulled a car onto the grass quadrangle between two BEQ high rise buildings, cranked up the stereo, and commenced enjoying their 4th of July holiday weekend with a cooler full of beer. This group included my ill-fated GSM2. More than a few beers were rapidly consumed in time-honored sailor fashion. One of the enlisted men assigned to the NAS Key West Shore Patrol happened by, and took exception to the festivities. (This sailor, we later learned, had a history of complaints against him for racial bias and excessive force.) He was on duty, so was armed with a badge, a nightstick, a service revolver and the cloak of authority. He ordered the men to move the car back into the parking lot. My GSM2, quite uncharacteristically, spoke up and took exception to this. An argument ensued, during which the Shore Patrolman threatened to take my sailor into custody of he did not comply. Well, he did not. So the SP attempted to restrain and arrest my sailor, all by himself. The GSM2 was tall, wiry and fairly fit, so this ill-advised effort quickly went south and a scuffle ensued during which my sailor somehow disarmed the SP of his revolver. Whoops. All stop!

The SP raised his hands and backed away to the end of the quadrangle courtyard between the buildings, where he got on his radio and called for backup. My inebriated GSM2, looking down the courtyard, saw him stop departing, and cranked off a round in his general direction, then emptied the other five rounds into the ground, threw the pistol across the grass, and sat down at a picnic bench to have another beer. The SP, seeing that my man was now unarmed, went to his personal vehicle in the BEQ parking lot, retrieved a personally-owned .357 Magnum revolver, and running up to my now-unarmed and placid GSM2, placed the cocked revolver against his head and threatened to blow his brains out if he moved. He thereby successfully took him into custody.

I was able to visit my sailor in the NAS Key West Brig a few hours later. Sobered up, he was depressed and fairly uncommunicative. He was in serious trouble, and was certain to face a court-martial. If convicted, this would be a federal felony, a crime of violence, and a conviction which would affect the rest of his life. About all I could do was to ensure that he was assigned a competent JAG Corps defense attorney, that he was being fairly treated and had what necessities he required while in the Brig, and to wish him luck with his defense. Unfortunately, I have no idea how this turned out, as I departed Key West long before the man went to trial. His defense attorney was made aware of the history of racial bias /excessive force complaints against the SP. Even so, I can't imagine it went well for him.

CHAPTER 33

Running Down the Wind

In the early fall of 1988, I experienced one of the most exhilarating transits of my entire career. My *Oliver Hazard Perry*-class Guided Missile Frigate *USS MAHLON S. TISDALE* (FFG-27) was tasked to spend some time in Nanoose Bay, British Columbia, at the Canadian Forces Maritime Experimental Test Range (CFMETR). This instrumented test range is where new torpedoes and other underwater technologies are evaluated. We had recently completed our refresher training in Pearl Harbor, HI, and had done quite well in the Anti-Submarine Warfare exercises associated with that training (including beating the stuffing out of a PACFLEET

Los Angeles-class fast attack submarine in a simulated shallow-water exercise, described in Chapter 28: "The Knife Fight.") Not long after that performance, we were approached by representatives of the Navy office which was at the time working on the development of a new advanced lightweight torpedo, the Mark 50 ALWT. They were scheduled to perform some of the early operational testing of that new weapon, and wondered if we would like to be the firing platform for the testing. They explained that they had chosen us because they were convinced that we would do a good job of targeting and firing the new fish, based upon our recent performance off of Pearl Harbor. They wanted no "operator error" to contribute to the statistics recorded for the new program. We were honored to be asked, and eagerly agreed to perform the service.

The testing went well, we did as we were asked to do, and fun was had by all for several days as we shot several new prototype surface-fired torpedoes at exercise targets. This is where the tale begins. Since we had squeezed this effort into our operating schedule, we now had to make up lost time and get back to our home port of San Diego, and back on schedule to meet our other commitments. We bid a fond farewell to the Pacific Northwest, and in a demanding multi-hour navigation detail, transited the Straits of Georgia and Juan De Fuca, passed Cape Flattery and turned south towards California.

My Commanding Officer authorized the ship to use full speed during our transit, once we were in safe waters and risk of collision with other vessels was reduced. This was a thrill, as we did not usually go quite that fast unless something pressing was requiring us to do so. So we rang up full bells and set off at thirty knots. Once we passed Cape Flattery, and into the Pacific Ocean proper, things got very interesting. A major storm had passed through the area in the few days before our departure. It had left large southerly seas and 30 knot winds in its wake. We now were running down those winds and surfing down those seas, hauling ass at full speed. As Officer of the Deck, I was stunned to walk out on the bridge wing and feel NO APPARENT WIND at a full bell. We were going south at 30 knots, the wind was blowing south at 30 knots, and the bridge wing was eerily calm, the flags overhead barely flapping at all on their halyards. I've never felt that, before or since.

Then another factor made things even more interesting. The bad weather of the past few days had apparently hit a coastal freighter or barge carrying a topside load of large logs, felled timber being taken to a lumber mill. The vessel had spilled its entire load of logs into the ocean, and these enormous waterlogged behemoths were now floating all along our prescribed track, bobbing in the big seas. They were low in the water, very hard to see, and in no predictable spacing or orientation relative to our track. Hitting one of them could easily damage our sonar dome, our propeller, our fin stabilizers, and possibly even our hull. I called the Captain and reported the hazard. He ordered me to continue at full speed, but to do whatever I needed to do to avoid hitting any of the logs. I was given *carte blanche* to maneuver as necessary. I took the Conn from a more junior officer, stationed myself on the starboard bridge wing, and enjoyed one of the most exciting shiphandling watches of my career. We passed the word to all hands over the 1MC general announcing system, *"Stand by for heavy rolls and unpredictable turns."* We would see a log ahead, and I would order the rudder turned to move the ship enough to miss it. Sometimes this was a gentle correction, barely felt below decks. Other times, it required a full rudder turn, with the ship heeling over and shuddering as it changed course violently.

On one of these maximum turns, we heard a crash from below decks, where the Supply Department was getting ready to serve dinner. I received an irate telephone call from the Supply Officer, berating me for having just broken a large stack of china plates on the mess decks. With the Boatswains Mate of the Watch holding the phone to my ear, while I gripped the bridge railing, I invited him to come up to the bridge and see what all the commotion was for, reminded him of the importance of "securing for sea" and explained that we had meant what we said when we passed the word. He politely declined my invitation to see what bridge watchstanding was like at the moment. After a few hours (and thankfully before sunset!), we had passed through the log danger area. We continued on course and speed for a couple of days, making the fastest transit I ever made on a conventional ship and reaching our home port in record, welcome time.

CHAPTER 34

Tiger Cruise!

One of the more fun evolutions that Navy ships get to experience once in a while is the "Tiger Cruise." This is a period of otherwise low-risk transit, during which crew members are allowed to invite relatives aboard, to see and experience Navy life firsthand. There are age and medical fitness restrictions, of course, and in my day, Tigers could only be male, as combatant-ship crews were all-male. (I can't imagine how difficult it must be today, bringing teenage girls, young sisters and wives aboard ships with hundreds of sailors returning from 7-month deployments. I'm glad I don't have to manage it.) Many a modern sailor first caught the "I want to join the Navy" bug on a Tiger Cruise, and it is a valuable recruiting tool, while also letting family members see what their loved one does when they are away for those long periods. Obviously, berthing spaces are at a premium, so some crew members are allowed to take shore leave, freeing up some bunks. Other members sometimes share their bunks with their guests, by "hotbunking" (one is awake while the sleeps in the bunk.) Cot space is made in odd corners. Sailors still stand their watches and perform their other duties, but they then can spend some free time showing their "Tigers" around the ship.

My first ship hosted a memorable Tiger Cruise in summer 1985, as we and our Battle Group transited back to San Diego, CA from Pearl Harbor, HI at the end of our Indian Ocean deployment. Most of the other ships in the BG did the same thing, so much effort was made to bring the ships into a tight formation, so that all ships would be visible to each other during daylight hours. Drills were performed, allowing guests to see signal flags, flashing light, precision maneuvering drills, battle exercises, and even some small arms weapons firing. Carrier planes and helicopters flew overhead, in some cases LOW overhead. One F-14 Tomcat went supersonic right above my cruiser, rattling the bridge windows and shaking dust, paint chips and an old rusty set of pliers out of the cabling in the overhead of the bridge! That was a memorable **BOOM!** The Carrier Air Wing put on a tremendous show for the tight formation, flying by in formations, and in some cases, dropping live ordnance, making huge bomb explosions and flashes. This was all done using training ordnance expenditure; you have to drop bombs once in a while to stay certified to do so. So the Airedales saved up some training exercises and performed them while everyone could watch! The surface ships likewise did some gun shoots for the same purpose. It was a blast showing USN combat capability to our guests, young and old. We had sons, nephews, brothers, fathers and at least one grandfather that I know of. Most of them had a great time, although some discovered firsthand what seasickness is all about. (Believe me, that is the sickest sick you never want to experience. It goes on for days, you know it is unlikely to end any time soon, and at times you are afraid that you AREN'T going to die....it's that uncomfortable, if you are prone to it.)

Another point of pride for the Tiger Cruise was Navy chow! The Supply departments did their best to serve hot, delicious meals. The kids LOVED the ever-flowing "bug juice" (like Kool-Aid, but in Navy parlance) dispensers and there were frequent visits to the soft-serve ice cream machines! Card and board games, movie showings, and general educational events all played a part in making the time pass. All in all, it was a fantastic experience for most of the Tigers, and we enjoyed having them aboard, seeing our own shipboard service through fresh, unaccustomed eyes. If you ever get the chance to go on one of these, I heartily recommend that you take it.

CHAPTER 35

Why We Post a Shore Patrol

One of the stereotypes of the sailor on "liberty", as temporary absence from the ship for in-port recreation is called, is misbehavior. Say it ain't so, but sailors have for millennia amassed a well-deserved reputation for partying hard when they are allowed to go ashore. If you ever visit a warship and see what their normal duties and surroundings are when working aboard ship, you will perhaps understand and forgive them for some of this excess abandon.

In an effort to keep things under some semblance of control, ships post a Shore Patrol of crew members, uniformed with SP armbands and usually armed with nightsticks, whose job it is to rein in (and if necessary, forcibly return to the ship) errant members of the crew whose judgement has fallen short of expected requirements. Sometimes the shenanigans can be hilarious.

One one port visit near the end of an Indian Ocean deployment, my Guided Missile Frigate was visiting Phuket, Thailand. (Get your mind out of the gutter, that is pronounced "Poo-ket.") This beautiful, tropical beach resort city is world-famous for adult recreation of many types. Among its many amenities were featured motorcycle rentals, jet ski rentals, sailboat rentals, parasailing, snorkeling, scuba diving, and bar after bar after bar, all filled with single Thai ladies. We anchored out, as there were no dockside berths suitable for our use. Our visit coincided with a major Thai cultural event, the Songkran, or "Water Festival."

Songkran is Thailand's most famous festival. An important event on the Buddhist calendar, this water festival marks the beginning of the traditional Thai New Year. The name Songkran comes from a Sanskrit word meaning 'passing' or 'approaching'. Basically, everyone walks around throwing water on everyone else. In a beach resort like Phuket, this results in the world's largest wet t-shirt contest featuring the hundreds of lovely Thai girls as incidental competitors. Needless to say, our crew was very excited to take part.

We arranged for large teak passenger ferries to come alongside our ship and take crew members in from the anchorage. They later transferred to a wooden "longtail" speedboat, for the final leg to the white sand beach. Before we let the first liberty section go, the Captain gave a stern briefing to all hands aboard. He gave explicit orders that NO MOTORCYCLES were to be ridden and NO JET SKIS were to be rented. These were restrictions placed by Commander, Pacific Fleet, in response to numerous injuries and money extortion scams perpetrated on sailors. We then let the liberty section go and continued to anchor the ship and get things shut down for a multi-day port visit.

About 30 minutes after the first ferry departed with its cargo of liberty hounds, my First Lieutenant (a Master Chief Boatswain's Mate) had a detail of his division on the forecastle, adjusting the anchor rig to the precise settings we desired for a safe anchorage. Out of the blazing sun three small, buzzing, mosquito-like objects appeared on the bay. They were jet skis! And they were closing the ship at high speed. In a few moments they were upon us, buzzing the ship and whooping it up....and being ridden by three of his Deck Division's junior sailors! The Master Chief just waved his hands, and shouted orders to them to return to shore and report directly to the Shore Patrol, immediately. They were back aboard and forbidden to go ashore again for the duration of the port visit within an hour!

After a few hours, all was settled down and the Captain felt comfortable going ashore. As he was walking down the main street of beachside Phuket, here came a motorcycle, being ridden at low speed by a stunning Thai girl in a bikini top and white hot pants.....with the ship's Anti-Submarine Warfare Officer riding pillion behind her! The Captain literally reached out as they passed, grabbed the ASWO by the collar and dragged him off the bike. His sea-lawyerly defense of *"I didn't RENT that bike, and I wasn't DRIVING it, Captain!"* cut no ice with the CO. He was likewise sent back to the ship, not to return ashore for the duration.

The next night, I was going ashore, and I was told that the SPs had a problem. One of the men of my department, a Third Class Boatswain's Mate, was injured, inebriated and refusing to be taken into custody by the SPs and brought back to the ship. Now this guy was special. He was a consummate seaman, one of the best Boatswain's Mates I ever knew. When things were dicey, this was the guy you wanted on the scene, handling the problem with the replenishment rig or the anchor or mooring tackle. He was knowledgeable, brave and skilled. I'd seen him do some hair-raising things that could easily have gotten a lesser man killed. The problem was, he was a quintessential blue collar, hard-drinking bad boy. He just got into trouble a lot, losing a stripe each time, shrugging it off as the cost of living his life and carrying on. In my time aboard the ship, I saw him make and lose several stripes. He would take the exam, excel and get promoted, and then get reduced in rank at a Captain's Mast, to start over again. One decoration he was unlikely to ever earn was the Good Conduct medal.

I grabbed a Hospital Corpsman (medic) and took him and his aid bag with me to the bar where the ruckus was reported to be taking place. Sure enough, there was my Boatswain's Mate, sitting on a chair, drunk and bleeding from a pretty severe cut to one hand. He had been playing pool, and had hit his head on the tiffany-style lamp hanging low over the pool table, ruining his shot. No problem! He simply rammed his fist through the lamp, breaking the glass and gashing his hand in the process. And no, he WASN'T going to abandon his game of pool to return to the ship. His Shore Patrol shipmates liked this guy too, and they weren't in the mood to issue him some hickory shampoo with their nightsticks to gain his compliance. That's why they called me. So I sat down with him, and we talked things over a bit. He was still rip-snorting drunk, so some of the conversation was him interjecting in gutter Spanish. I was able to get him to let the Corpsman stitch up his hand, sitting right on the pool table. And enough time went by that he sobered up enough to calm down and agree to call it a night. We assured the bartender that his damages would be paid for (and they were). A report had to be filed, so the Captain had no choice but to take a stripe from him at a subsequent Captain's Mast. (The guy made his rank back within 6 months. I swear, we should have just put Velcro on his uniform sleeves and rating insignia.)

CHAPTER 36

Crossing The Line

One of the more ancient traditions followed by mariners for centuries is that of holding initiation ceremonies when crossing the Equator. Called "Crossing The Line" ceremonies, these events are a throwback to centuries past, when sailors had a bit more free rein to test new hands, and coincidentally, to have a bit of fun at their expense. These were elaborate hazing rituals, steeped in tradition. The fact is that on a few occasions across the centuries, the festivities have gotten out of hand, and there are a few recorded instances of serious indignities, injuries and even a few deaths having occurred among the various fleets around the world. (Since the advent of putting women on USN ships, the traditional Crossing The Line ceremonies have been significantly watered down and scaled back, lest someone be offended and complain. In my opinion, this is not progress.) I will describe what the experience was like at my initiation on January 10th 1985.

A sailor who has already been initiated through a Crossing The Line ceremony is called a "Shellback." This professional mariner has thereby proven himself to be tough, resilient and respectful of tradition and possessed of a sense of humor. This is a nautical being worthy of some respect. He has been admitted into the Solemn Mysteries of the Order of Shellbacks by the personal order of His Majesty King Neptune, Ruler of the Raging Main. Having once earned this distinction, he need never undergo this trying process of admittance ever again. Once a Shellback, always a Shellback. On the other hand, a sailor who has not formally been granted admission into the Realm of King Neptune is termed a "Pollywog", or "Slimy Pollywog", if you prefer. This is a pitiful creature, untried, unproven, ignorant, and unworthy to walk upright among his Shellback shipmates. He has not yet earned admittance into the maritime realm upon which he travels and works only through the forbearance of King Neptune. He must gain this formal admission by passing through an arduous process of examination.

I was awakened well before dawn on the day my first ship crossed the equator for the first time on our deployment to the western Pacific, at coordinates Latitude 00 degrees 00 minutes N / Longitude 105 degrees 35 minutes E (this is a point in the Indian Ocean, southwest of Sumatra, Indonesia.) Two Shellbacks (enlisted men assigned to my Signals Division) appeared at my stateroom door and pounded on it like sledgehammers. I was ordered to put on my uniform clothing, but with the trousers and shirt on inside out and backwards, with underwear worn over the clothing vice under it (also inside out and backwards), and with socks worn inside out, with the trousers tucked inside them. I was made aware of my status as a lowly Pollywog, and instructed not to address any Shellback unless spoken to, and to avoid making eye contact with so lofty a being. I was ordered to crawl on hands and knees, as I was unworthy of walking among true seaman. I joined over a hundred of my fellow Pollywog shipmates, all dressed in the same fashion, as we were not-too-gently herded onto the forecastle (the foredeck) of the ship, up at the pointy end. This herding process was encouraged through the liberal application of "shillelaghs" (pronounced, "Shillaylees") in the hands of the Shellbacks. These are about 15" lengths of rubber-lined cotton-jacketed 1.5-inch firehose, with one end duct taped into a rudimentary handle. (When gently applied, these are unlikely to cause injury; sort of like a spanking from a parent who doesn't really want to spank you.)

On the foredeck, some well-meaning Shellback had smeared the contents of a 5 gallon can of cooking lard all over the forecastle. (I learned later that our appearance-obsessed Captain, the legendary Screamer of previous Sea Stories, just about popped an artery when he learned of this. Significant efforts were made to degrease the ship later in the day.) We all crawled into a tightly-packed mass in the darkness while Shellbacks played cold seawater over us through firehoses, shouting orders and critical "encouragement" for us to sing, make marine animal noises, and generally debase ourselves. The lard made crawling to our positions on the sloping forecastle somewhat difficult, and certainly made an unusual first coat of what became an encrustation of other emollients as the day wore on. This lovely beginning lasted probably about an hour and was broken up as the sun rose over the calm ocean. I remember that it rained, a lovely, tropical Indian Ocean shower, which both warmed us and rinsed us of some of the salt.

We were then formed into line and ordered to crawl on the deck around the ship in a counterclockwise direction. This ship was 533 feet in length, so a lap around the ship was not trivial.

Exposed steel deck was coated with a thick layer of deck gray non-skid paint. This practically left your palms tattooed and your knees sore in short order. The shillelagh herding process continued. Every so often a nautical question would be asked, and if one did not know the right answer, a punishment might be levied. I remember one shipmate being told to lie on deck, put his head though a mooring chock extended outboard, and loudly call for Flipper the Dolphin to come to his assistance. (Flipper never came, obviously having better things to do.) We were eventually assigned duties. I was assigned to stand by in the galley as meals were prepared. Bring sacks of potatoes, open cans, wash dishes, or take bags of trash to the stern. Etc. Others got other assignments. The day wore on.

In the afternoon, the actual ceremonies got underway. The ship's bell rang ten times (the usual maximum for the most senior of officers is eight), and the arrival of King Neptune and his court was announced over the 1MC general announcing system. King Neptune (an older Warrant Officer member of the crew) was resplendent in his imperial robes, complete with a flowing white fake beard and of course he carried his trident. He was accompanied by Queen Amphitrite and several sirens (crew members in outlandish mermaid-esque drag) and by a cast of other costumed characters including the Royal Doctor, Royal Dentist, and Royal Baby. He demanded to know by whose authority the embarked Pollywogs passed through his realm. And when he learned that we were there seeking his approval, King Neptune ordered his court to assemble on the helo deck aft, and for the trials to begin. He took his seat on a throne at the end of a line of several members of his court. Each Pollywog in turn made his way to the line, on hands and knees, first passing through a long wood-framed plastic-lined tunnel, which had been filled with all the garbage scraps from a couple of days' worth of galley meals, cooking oil, seawater, and who knows what else. It reeked and was thoroughly unpleasant. Did I mention that one had to squirm through it on one's belly, and occasionally roll completely over in it? Suffice it to say, when a Pollywog exited the tunnel, he was thoroughly coated in noxious effluent. The Royal Dentist first examined his teeth, and administered some dental hygiene assistance (a squirt of a garlic and hot pepper sauce from a plastic squirt bottle. The Royal Doctor then had a look, and pronounced the Pollywog fit for duty, but only after having administered some deep-sea medicine (a spoonful of castor oil.) The Royal Baby was next. This was the most obese crew member available, dressed in a diaper and with a large pacifier hanging about his neck. His prodigious belly was smeared with some kind of grease, and each Pollywog was grabbed by the ears and had his face rubbed in the greasy mess. Finally, each man appeared before King Neptune, and was adjudged to have been found worthy of admittance into the Solemn Mysteries of the Order of Shellbacks. He was ordered to arise and was welcomed into the ancient company of professional mariners, now and forever pronounced a Shellback.

When all of this was over, it was time to clean up. Someone had thoughtfully rigged a 2.5" firehose with a 12-foot aviation firefighting applicator nozzle, forming a forceful cold seawater shower, right on the forward corner of the flight deck. Most of us felt that the working uniform we had been wearing for the day was totally ruined, and simply stripped it off and threw it over the side, then showered naked in the bracing salt water, getting the first coat of goo washed away. We would have a hot freshwater shower later. Freshly cleaned and re-uniformed, we new Shellbacks resumed our shipboard duties as full-fledged maritime professionals. Once all was done, everything was disassembled, stowed or discarded and the ship thoroughly cleaned from all traces of the event. We had Crossed the Line.

Note: While I saw nothing untoward happen on my Crossing The Line Initiation, it's easy to see how things could get out of hand if not properly supervised. I did notice that throughout my day as a Pollywog, there was always some member of my Division nearby, apparently keeping watch over me to make sure that some other Shellback shipmate did not take undue advantage of the opportunity to heap excess abuse on an officer. I appreciated the gesture then, and remember it now with some pride, as it speaks to the regard which my men and I held each other in. It made even more sense to me a few years later, when as a Shellback I participated in a similar ceremony aboard another ship. That ship's wardroom had among its members a young Ensign, a recent graduate of the US Naval Academy, who was a bit egotistical and who had unwisely made some comments indicating that he felt that officers were superior to mere enlisted men. That guy was herded mercilessly with considerable shillelagh attention, all day long. When he showered on deck at the end of the process, his butt was so badly bruised and reddened from the beating that the ship's corpsman took note and had him drop by sickbay for a closer examination to make sure that he was not actually injured. I gather that he learned a bit of humility from the experience.

CHAPTER 37

Collateral Duties

One of the banes of existence for a junior US Navy line officer is the concept of "Collateral Duties." These are additional responsibilities given to an officer, to perform in his so-called (often mythical) "spare time." Often, these jobs consume far more of an officer's attention than might be expected.

What exactly does a Navy junior officer (JO) do, anyway? Each young officer assigned to a ship is expected to perform several functions. First and foremost, he is assigned as a Division Officer, the first-line officer supervisor of a functional grouping of enlisted sailors. (A Division is analogous to a Platoon in Army/Marine parlance.) His division will be part of a larger Department of sailors; on a typical combatant ship these departments comprise Operations, Weapons (now called Combat Systems), Engineering and Supply (although line officers do not work in the Supply department, Supply Corps officers do.) To help him in leading his division (and in fact to teach him his trade and the basics of leadership,) he is "assisted" by a senior enlisted man, usually a Chief Petty Officer (E-7) or above. Depending upon the size of his division, he may have more than one CPO, but one of them will be designated as the Leading CPO, his primary enlisted advisor. The young officer is responsible for the welfare, training, performance and discipline of his men. He writes their performance evaluations and keeps the chain of command informed of all matters pertaining to his Division's responsibilities. Typically, a Division has well-defined mission function. Communications Division, for example, would be comprised of Radiomen, and part of the Operations Department.

In addition to this formal job assignment, the JO is also assigned numerous additional, or "Collateral" duties. Some of these don't take much effort. Others are very time consuming. For example:

CMS Custodian: responsible for inventory, issuance, control and destruction of all shipboard communications and other cryptographic material. This may include Nuclear Weapons Control materials, for ships equipped to carry them, whether or not such weapons are actually aboard or not. This is a big one, and a ZERO DEFECTS job. One screwup can get you cashiered.

Intelligence Officer: maintains custody of classified publications, gives the Commanding Officer daily intel briefs when deployed. Conducts intelligence reporting when something of interest happens by.

Laundry Officer. Yes, I'm not joking.

Morale, Welfare and Recreation Officer. Tries to think of things to improve morale. Plans sporting events, movie nights, special tours and events when in a liberty port, holiday celebrations. Maintains inventory of baseball bats and gloves, soccer balls, boxing gloves, etc.

Wardroom Mess Caterer. Develops and proposes the menus and decorations and special events for the officers' wardroom mess. This walks a fine line between food quality and cost. (Officers personally pay for their food in the USN; enlisted men's meals are paid for as part of their enlistment contract.) The Wardroom can have steak and lobster every night, but the bill will be enormous and no one will be happy. Ditto franks and beans every night: cheap, but a mutiny maker for sure. Bottom line is, the Mess Caterer can't please everyone and is usually being criticized by somebody. It's a thankless task.

Wardroom Mess Treasurer: Actually bills officers and collects their monthly mess payments, transferring funds to the supply department to cover the costs incurred. This includes visiting officers and certain civilians who are temporarily assigned to the ship and welcomed to the wardroom mess commensurate with their status. A relentless pursuer of mess bill scofflaws. Must maintain careful records and ledgers, undergo periodic audits. Another thankless task.

The Bull Ensign: The most senior of the most junior officers on the ship. This Ensign usually wears a set of oversize gold bar rank insignia, engraved "BULL" to indicate his "seniority". He is expected to ride herd over the other Ensigns in the wardroom, keeping their decorum and humility within due bounds. He is happy to pass these rank insignia off to the next-most-senior Ensign when he makes Lieutenant Junior Grade (LTJG).

The "George" Ensign: The most junior Ensign aboard, the newest, greenest officer in the Wardroom. Traditionally called "George" to his face, he is the recipient of much verbal and practical abuse (all in good fun, of course.) Something not very pleasant, menial, or humiliating needs to be done by an officer? Call "George!" He is EXCEPTIONALLY happy when a more junior Ensign reports aboard and assumes the title.

Movie Officer: Selects what movie (nowadays a DVD, in my day, a reel-to-reel projector film) is shown in the wardroom each night. Is under constant pressure to select films everyone wants to watch (explosions and female nudity being a plus!) Another "can't please everyone" thankless job.

Mess Sample Officer. This one is rotated, not a permanent collateral duty. By regulation, EVERY meal served on the mess deck to enlisted crew members must be sampled for quality, taste and appearance. Some officer must sample a bit of each one, inspect the serving line and mess decks themselves to make sure the crew is being properly fed and cared for.

Small Arms Custodian: maintains control and inventory of all the small arms (pistols, rifles, shotguns, perhaps light machine guns) assigned to the ship. Another ZERO DEFECTS career killer if screwed up.

Needless to say, the modern USN JO is a busy creature, with plenty to keep him occupied.

CHAPTER 38

Gundecking

The US Navy is, among other things, a soul-crushing bureaucracy. Administrative paperwork is elaborate, often antiquated, and seemingly the first priority of all priorities, except perhaps the Holy Grail of 21st Century military service: "diversity and inclusion." Combat readiness and actual seamanship expertise rank far behind political correctness and paperwork in order of importance. (Author's Note: Take a look at the news over the last few years, documenting serious Navy mishaps. This is detrimental to our country's defense, and hopefully may be rectified in some future, clearer-thinking age. But I'm not holding my breath.)

The reality of shipboard service is that there are far too many tasks and requirements to be accomplished in any 24-hour day, and the marine environment, the press of work commitments and the limits of human endurance simply make it impossible to accomplish everything that the system demands to be done. So sailors, with too much to do and pressured to have their paperwork in perfect order, sometimes resort to falsifying records – a practice known as "Gundecking."

What kind of paperwork, you may ask? In my active duty and reserve service, there were several administrative systems which were intended to serve readiness needs, but which became the petty tyrant masters of all who served under them. One of these was the Planned Maintenance System (PMS.) The theory behind PMS was sound. Each piece of equipment should be maintained periodically, to ensure that it is operable when needed. So some committee of geniuses sat down and determined what maintenance actions ought to be performed, how, by whom, and how often.

Each action was then categorized according to periodicity. Daily, weekly, monthly, quarterly, semi-annually or annually. A Maintenance Requirement Card was prepared indicating what skill level was needed to perform the task, what tools and supplies would be needed to do it properly, and approximately how long the maintenance action should take. This MRC card then listed in excruciating order, how the task was intended to be performed. Step. By. Step. (I should note at this point that the PMS System was first developed in response to a US Air Force requirement and was presented to the USAF for adoption. The USAF said "hell, no, this is way too unwieldy and burdensome. No thanks." The Navy then adopted it. No kidding.)

Preventative maintenance sounds good, right? Well, in practice, this became a self-licking ice cream cone. Because PMS schedules, records and tasks became INSPECTABLE, with poor grades being assessed for minor infractions, bookkeeping errors, or missing scheduled maintenance actions due to the press of other business. These grades factor into performance evaluations and awards. So there was considerable pressure for the paperwork to look great. For example, let's say that a particular piece of equipment required disassembly, inspection, cleaning, lubrication and reassembly. The system says it has to be done monthly. The task ought to be performed by a E-3 Fireman in an associated occupational rating. All of these aspects are important, inspectable priorities. But perhaps the system is being operated, so can't be taken off-line to maintain it, or perhaps there are other things requiring the Division's time that week. Or perhaps no fully-qualified technician is available. You can see how reality intrudes. So the work center supervisor might find himself making record entries indicating that that piece of equipment (which is online and working flawlessly) was maintained properly, on schedule, by the right man. But then the PMS Inspection rears its ugly head. Shipboard supervisors are required to perform periodic checks to ensure that maintenance was done, and occasionally, a team of inspectors descends on the ship and audits the records, looking for discrepancies. And they perform the dreaded "spot check." The records say Fireman Finorky did this maintenance two months ago. "OK, Let's see Finorky's training records; is he qualified? Show me the man. Well, hello, Fireman Finorky! Grab your PMS card for this particular check, and show me exactly how you do/did it." And if Finorky has a bad day, or makes a mistake, or doesn't explain well, or is just a muttonhead, that check is failed and your grade suffers greatly.

Another rich environment rife with Gundecking? The Personnel Qualification System (PQS.) For each significant task aboard ship, some big brain sat down and determined what a person needed to know or be able to do to accomplish it. These were listed in a softcover PQS book for that task, which was issued to the new man. That person went through the PQS book and tried to learn each task, either through book study or hands-on training by an accomplished shipmate who was qualified to do it. And when the shipmate decided that the man knew what he was supposed to know for that line item, he affixed his signature to that line. When the book was full of signatures on every applicable line, the man was examined by some senior supervisor, who signed the book, and the man was now officially qualified. The problem? Well, these books are GENERAL in content. Ships are SPECIFIC, and systems vary greatly between ship types, classes and variants. Some qualified personnel aren't great at administrative tasks, some are nearing the end of their enlistments and couldn't give less of a rat's ass about affixing their signature to someone's book, and memory fades in the time it takes to complete some books. And again, records are kept and are INSPECTABLE. Another self-licking ice cream cone.

The worst case of Gundecking I ever saw was during my first year aboard my first ship. The ship was undergoing a one-year baseline overhaul. This is an extended period of very thorough repair and refurbishment, performed by a shipyard. And of the many thousands of tasks to be accomplished, some are allotted to the shipyard, some to the actual manufacturers of installed equipment, and some to the crew itself, called the "Ship's Force." Renovating a berthing compartment, for example, might be assigned to the Ship's Force.

Now, all of these maintenance tasks need to be finished by the overhaul completion date, and some need to be completed in time to support other actions which depend upon them; for example, that berthing compartment needs to be completed before crew move-aboard date, to support the first post-overhaul sea trials. And to keep progress generally on schedule, keep the crew busy, and keep the brass happy, general, steady progress needs to be shown. Enter the Ships Force Overhaul Management System, also known as SFOMS. In this masterpiece of military industrial bureaucracy, each work center of each Division of the ship's crew was tasked to accomplish particular jobs, and to submit WEEKLY reports showing their progress on their assigned tasks. "Job #1098 is 14% complete today." With details. Etc. And the statistics generated by these reports were scrutinized by senior leadership, shipyard managers, and the larger Navy bureaucracy to make sure the ship was doing its job properly. I was given the unenviable task of supervising the collection and data entry of these weekly reports from every work center of a 900-man ship's crew. I was (ta-DAH!) the SFOMS Coordinator.

So, my ambitious first Captain and his evil minions decided the best way to keep the Shipyard and Navy Brass happy....was to show them what they wanted to see. And every Division aboard the ship was ordered to submit weekly reports indicating that they were exactly on schedule for whatever tasks they were assigned to perform, regardless of the actual facts on the deckplates. "This is week #32 of the overhaul. We are 62% through the time allotted.

Job #1098 (B Division Berthing Overhaul) is 62% complete as of this date." Despite the fact that the Berthing Compartment renovation had not yet begun. Etc. It was all a colossal waste of time and a Gundecking masterpiece. Yet, somehow, the overhaul got done, we returned to sea and to duty on schedule and in fighting trim. So how necessary was it to saddle the crew with SFOMS reporting in the first place? The US Navy somehow never got around to asking that question.

Cumshaw Gold

CHAPTER 39

Cumshaw

A time-honored Navy tradition and method of getting what you need, when you need it, is the ancient practice known as "Cumshaw." This is basically bribery, offering an inducement in goods or services to the provider of something you need who does not have to meet your requirement, but who may then decide to do so. You provide something of value to someone, who then provides something of value to you. This may work as follows.

You need something from a particular work center aboard your ship. They are busy, so aren't particularly energized about providing your need immediately. So you offer to send over one of your junior enlisted men to help them in some menial tasks, easing their workload temporarily. And presto, you get what you need on an expedited basis. Cumshaw.

In my day, the gold standard of Cumshaw material was ground coffee. The Navy runs on coffee. No matter what anyone may say about nuclear power, jet fuel, diesel, or gasoline, ships and shore stations require prodigious quantities of hot coffee to function. Pretty much every work center, watch station and mess facility has one or more pots going, whenever work or watchstanding is being done. If some future enemy ever corners the global market on coffee beans and threatens war with the US Navy, capitulation will occur without a shot being fired. Navy coffee is traditionally prepared about double normal strength to that of a civilian supplier, and each pot has a pinch of salt added "to settle the grounds." THAT is what Navy coffee tastes like, at least in my day. What with the ongoing PC diversity, equity and inclusion wussification of the fleet, it is possible that Keurig cups of mocha-choka latte soymilk blech have found their way aboard ship, but I sincerely hope not. Keurig cups won't win our next sea battle.

Let's say that your ship is looking a little the worse for wear, and the Captain wants a new sparkling white overhead awning made for the Quarterdeck. These were traditionally made from white canvas, but today are probably constructed of a thick vinyl material called Herculite. The First Lieutenant (Deck Division officer) passes this requirement on to his Leading Chief Petty Officer (A Chief Boatswain's Mate,) who directs a less-senior petty officer to put in a work request with the Canvas Shop in whatever shore-side maintenance facility supports the ship. The word comes back that the Shop is fully booked, and filling this requirement will likely take 1-2 months. The Captain is not going to be best pleased, and everyone knows what happens when the Captain isn't pleased. So the Chief Boatswain's Mate, takes a little walk over to the Canvas Shop with a seabag over his shoulder. He speaks privately with the Chief Petty Officer who supervises the Shop. Mystical incantations and secret signs known only to initiated Chief Petty Officers are exchanged, and a couple of #10 cans of ground coffee change hands. The Canvas Shop guy works a bit longer that evening, on his "personal time", or perhaps a subordinate is assigned extra duty for some infraction. Either way, the work gets done, a sparking new awning appears on your ship within a few days, the Canvas Shop has a supply of hot coffee for the next week or two, and the Captain is pleased. Cumshaw wins again.

An even older tradition of Cumshaw used to be practiced aboard ships back when daily rum rations occurred.

> "The UK Navy rum ration, or "tot", from 1850 to 1970 consisted of one-eighth of an imperial pint (71 ml) of rum at 95.5 proof (54.6% ABV), given out to every sailor at midday. Senior ratings (petty officers and above) received their rum neat, whilst for junior ratings it was diluted with two parts of water to make three-eighths of an imperial pint (213 ml) of grog.[1] The rum ration was served from one particular barrel, also known as the "Rum Tub", which was ornately decorated and was made of oak and reinforced with brass bands with brass letters saying "The Queen, God Bless Her".

Note that the rum ration was only stopped on 31 July 1970 in the UK Royal Navy, and it lasted until 1990 in the Royal New Zealand Navy! Spirit rations were important to morale in an age when sea service was arduous, painful, and dangerous. The alcohol basically helped anesthetize a sailor who spent much of his life cold, wet, sore, hungry and tired. So a sailor's rum ration was a valuable commodity which could be traded for other things of value, like standing a watch in his stead, or ironing his uniform, or making him a fancy knotwork lanyard for his Boatswain's Pipe. And as all services rendered were not of equal value, the inducement offered was likewise graduated. A shipmate's rum ration might be apportioned in several ways:

"Wetters" – you could just drink enough to wet your lips for a flavor of rum.

"Sippers" – you could take a sip, but not a full drink.

"Gulpers" – you could take a full gulp of rum or grog, enough to make your Adam's Apple bob once.

"Halfers" – you got exactly half of the man's daily ration

Or you might be traded the entire draught of rum or grog.

Old ways got to be old ways by being effective. And sailors usually find a way to get the job done.

Firefighting

CHAPTER 40
Firefighting and Damage Control Training

Navy ships are first and foremost fighting machines, equipped and intended to engage in mortal combat. And when engaged in that contact sport, is it all-too-likely that you are going to take as well as give battle damage. The Navy therefore sets great store by being prepared and trained to conduct firefighting and damage control operations. Many sailors attend formal firefighting and damage control training schools.

A Navy ship is essentially a big metal box, full of lethal things, and living sailors. Fire inside the box is incredibly bad juju. Just look at this past year's news reports of a catastrophic fire aboard *USS BONHOMME RICHARD* (LHD-6). She is now severely damaged, and unlikely to ever sail again. She will cost $4 BILLION to replace. Other historic ship fires which occasioned many losses of lives include USS FORRESTAL, USS BELKNAP, and USS ENTERPRISE. None of these were occasioned by battle damage inflicted by an enemy.

A ship's crew is therefore her first line of defense with regards to firefighting. And the crew must be organized, equipped, trained and drilled to perform this task effectively. There are four basic types of fires, each requiring a different type of firefighting effort and agent.

- Class "A" – combustible solids, like paper, cardboard, mattresses, wood, and other conventional materials.

- Class "B" – flammable liquids, such as fuel oil, gasoline, lube oil, cooking oil, or hydraulic fluid.

- Class "C" – electrical fire, in an energized circuit.

- Class "D" – special metals, such as sodium, magnesium, aluminum. These burn at extremely high temperatures, and are self-oxidizing and therefore very difficult to extinguish.

The main firefighting effort on a ship centers around a team attacking the fire with a 1.5" or 2.5" seawater-charged firehose, with a heavy nozzle. (This may be augmented by special liquid agents to deal with Class B or D fires. A Class C fire is fought with a CO_2 extinguisher.) The charged firehose hose is stiff, heavy and unwieldy. Water itself weighs 8 pounds per gallon. A fire fighting team is actually two hoses, side by side. One fights the fire, the other keeps the fire and heat off the firefighting party with a

Damage Control

cooling spray screen of water. This is a brutal, hot, exhausting and dangerous affair. The nozzlemen and hosemen need great physical strength, stamina and courage to traverse up and down ladders and through hatchways, and to approach a blazing fire in a dark, smoke-filled compartment and do battle with it. Nozzlemen require frequent relief, so the shipmate behind them moves up and takes the nozzle and the nozzleman falls back to rest, taking a more rearward position on the hose. All of the party are wearing a heavy breathing apparatus, fire protective gear, boots and gloves. They are sweating profusely and working at a high rate of physical load.

Firefighting school simulates this environment on shore, by constructing multi-story metal structures similar in design to a ship's interior. Ladders, gratings, mesh catwalks, bulkheads, doorways, and bilges are all present, giving the students the same kinds of obstacles they will face on board ship. Diesel fuel pipes run throughout the trainer, and can be controlled to spray fuel to put the fire wherever it is wanted, and to graduate its severity. So a fire is lighted, and allowed to heat the metal structure to hundreds of degrees Fahrenheit and fill it with impenetrable smoke. The team is then sent inside to battle the blaze, under the watchful eye of instructors. It is as real as it can get. And I can tell you from personal experience, it is HOT. You can barely see a thing in the smoky, sooty darkness. All that is missing is the charred bodies of dead shipmates getting in the way. Now imagine doing it at sea, inside a ship full of flammables and explosives, and with no one manning shutoff valves if the fire gets too intense.

Damage control training is similar. A training facility (usually dubbed "USS BUTTERCUP") contains decks, hatches, doorways, pipes, flanges, and ladders, It is built inside a larger box, so that it can be flooded with cold water, quickly, simulating seawater ingress due to battle damage. Pipes can "rupture", flanges can cut loose, bulkheads can weaken and threaten collapse. A team is sent in, to deal with each type of damage. They patch pipes spraying water at high pressure. They plug holes in decks and bulkheads, shore up collapsing bulkheads, and pack leaking flanges. This must all be done quickly, before the compartment they are in floods so deeply that the ship "sinks". You are soaked to the skin, shivering, and in simulated theory, about to drown. And the most modern of these trainers can be made to list several degrees from level, adding a realistic feeling of a sinking ship. Motivation to succeed is certainly instilled by the experience. Now imagine doing it at sea, in the dark, deep inside the ship, with your ship sinking under you.

Eternal vigilance is the price of safety at sea. And Damage Control is a brutally physical business.

Author's note: the US Navy has not taken significant battle damage from enemy action since 1987 (*USS STARK* (FFG-31)) and 1988 (*USS SAMUEL B. ROBERTS* (FFG-58)). Both of those ships had all-male crews, and they still nearly lost their ships due to the severity of their damage. The US Navy has simply forgotten what it is to have to fight battle damage aboard their ships on a frequent basis, and has sacrificed damage control readiness in the interest of political correctness. It should be readily apparent to any person with a shred of intellectual integrity that a policy of manning combatant ships with as many as 20% female crewmembers who on average have 45% – 75% less upper body strength than their male counterparts is not a recipe for successful damage control under combat conditions. Greater losses will definitely result in our next major sea war. This is simply an indisputable fact.

CHAPTER 41
Helicopter Operations

Everyone is familiar with the concept of US Navy carrier aviation, if for no other reason than the 1986 blockbuster movie *Top Gun*. Another, lesser-known cinematic masterpiece illustrating the technical complexity and risks attendant to carrier aviation is the 1954 film *The Bridges at Toko Ri*, starring William Holden and Mickey Rooney. I highly recommend watching this movie when you can. It is excellent.

There is another, mostly unsung but very important facet of naval aviation: the small combatant helicopter detachment. Every cruiser, destroyer and frigate in the US Navy has the capability to embark one or two helicopters, usually MH-60

Seahawk aircraft. This flexible, capable helo offers tremendous advantages in ocean surveillance, and is the weapon of choice when hunting a submarine, as it allows the ship to remain far from that potent adversary while using the helo to help locate the sub, and then to drop homing torpedoes on it for the kill. The embarked helo also provides some useful transportation and logistic support capability.

Getting a fast-moving jet onto the deck of an aircraft carrier, in all weather and at night is obviously a very demanding task. When you meet a carrier pilot wearing his "wings of gold", be sure to extend him the proper degree of respect for his skill and not inconsiderable store of personal courage. But consider the fact that a carrier is a huge, relatively stable ship which rarely rolls, pitches or yaws severely. A frigate or destroyer is another matter entirely, as these relatively small, skinny fast ships do all of the above, pretty much all of the time, and in bad weather, to an extreme degree. And the flight deck of a surface combatant is a very small piece of real estate upon which to land, while avoiding crashing your rotor disk into any part of the ship.

So how do helo pilots manage to launch and recover from small combatants? Launching isn't the hard part, as the helicopter and the ship are initially moving together; the helo pilot picks the moment, pulls rotor pitch to create lift, and takes off, immediately establishing his own stable flight motion. But landing is a different matter. First, the pilot has to FIND his ship, a small moving speck in an enormous ocean. He then lines up behind the ship, on an angle of approach which the deck is designed for, at the proper altitude. He matches the ship's course and speed, which have been selected to minimize the motion of the ship (and therefore the flight deck.) The ship's flight deck has a number of lights of various colors which help the pilot to see the deck, and to visually recognize its motion, its outlines and specifically where he needs to set his bird down to prevent flying his rotors into the ship's structure. The pilot is also in radio communication with the Helicopter Control Officer aboard the ship. This officer directs the ship's crew and equipment in supporting the launch and recovery of the aircraft. He adjusts the lighting, directs the deck crew and coordinates all aspects of the landing from the ship's perspective. (I was the HCO for my Guided Missile Frigate. When doing this, I sat in a small booth on the back side of the helo hangar, overlooking the flight deck. When the helo hovered to land, his rotor tips were spinning about ten feet right in front of my face. Needless to say, I was always hopeful that the pilot was on his game that day, as a slight miscalculation of too-far-forward was likely to kill us both.)

When all is ready, the pilot moves into a stable hover above the center of the flight deck, and lowers a metal fitting on the end of a wire cable. A deck crewman has to stand under the hovering helo to first contact the wire with an electrically-grounded probe on a fiberglass pole, as the spinning rotors generate an electrical static charge which can easily kill a man if it is not first discharged to ground. You don't simply reach up and grab the wire, if you want to live. The wire is grounded, and the fitting is then inserted into a metal device called the Recovery Assist, Securing and Traversing (RAST) system, more commonly known to sailors as the "Bear Trap." This runs along a track in the deck, and can be moved from flight deck center to inside the helo hangar.

The helo is now tethered to the ship, but still hovering in flight. And when the pilot judges that the ship is momentarily as stable as it is going to be, he indicates readiness and the ship winches him down to the deck using a powered winch hauling in on the cable. When his wheels are on deck, the jaws of the "Bear Trap" close, locking the cable in place and firmly fastening the bird to the ship (hence the name "Bear Trap." And presto, the helo has landed. Once the rotors and tail pylon have been folded to reduce the size of the aircraft for storage, the RAST tows the helo into the hangar and the hangar door is closed.

Imagine doing this at night, in rainy weather and high seas. A tip of the hat to the helo aviators. "Wings of Gold" indeed.

Another typical evolution ships conduct is Helo In-flight Refueling (HIFR), which greatly extends the flight time of the helo. Rather than landing to refuel, the helo hovers over the deck and a refueling hose is connected to his fuel port (after suitable electrical grounding per the above.) He then hovers just off the ship's quarter, but above the water so that if he crashes, he doesn't crash onto the flight deck while pumping high-pressure jet fuel and causing a massive fire aboard the ship. And jet fuel is pumped into his fuel tanks at high pressure and speed as he matches the ship's course and speed through the water in a stable hover. When he is full, he ejects the probe and proceeds on whatever mission he was pursuing before refueling.

I once flew off and back onto my ship with a naval aviator who had played a small part in a historic cold-war drama. This was 1988, and he was nearing the end of a long US Navy Reserve career, still flying the obsolescent LAMPS Mark 1 *Sea Sprite* aircraft. But on October 27th, 1962, he had been flying above a Soviet Foxtrot-class diesel attack submarine, the *B-59*, at the height of the tensest moment of the Cuban Missile Crisis. The B-59 and several other Soviet diesel subs (each carrying one T-5 nuclear-tipped torpedo) were approaching the US Navy's ships which were blockading Cuba as a result of the detection of Soviet nuclear missiles which had been stationed there. The US Navy wanted to give these submarines the clear message that they were considered potentially hostile and that steps would be taken to defend against them if they did not surface and withdraw. As there was no other way to communicate with a submerged Russian submarine, the Secretary of Defense authorized the Navy to drop "Practice Depth Charges," grenade-sized explosives which were designed to simulate the real, lethal thing in training. The explosions were intended to tell the submerged submarines that it was time to go "anywhere but here."

My pilot hovered his helicopter above the *B-59*, and attempted to drop a PDC from the external launcher, onto the submerged sub. Nothing happened, as the PDC hung up in the launcher, as they sometimes did. **So our hero, thinking fast, passed control of the bird to his copilot, opened the door of the aircraft, leaned out over the Caribbean Sea and kicked the launcher several times until the PDC dropped free and sank, doing its thing at the proper depth. BOOM. Splash.** Years later, it was determined that the Captain of the *B-59* had believed that he was under genuine depth charge attack, and he had been out of communication with Moscow for several days. He gave orders and intended to LAUNCH HIS NUCLEAR-TIPPED TORPEDO at the Navy ships. This was only prevented by the veto of an embarked senior officer aboard the boat. The Cuban Missile Crisis might have had a much different ending, but for the good judgment and restraint of one Soviet naval officer.

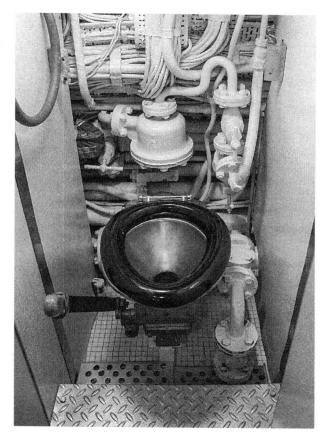

A Submarine Toilet

CHAPTER 42

Submarine Toilets

Have you ever wondered how a submarine manages the inevitable by-products of human life? A crew of 130-150 sailors, eating the finest meals served aboard any US Navy ship, generates significant quantities of sewage, which must be disposed of. And the ambient pressure of the ocean at the depths where the submarine operates is far too great for gravity drains or even mechanical pumps to overcome. So how do submariners get rid of the material which most other humans give little to no thought to, once it has "been eliminated?"

A submarine toilet is a relatively simple device. But it can occasion serious risk. Of course, space being at a premium aboard any submarine, toilet compartments are built as small as possible. The toilet bowl is a sturdy, stainless-steel affair, topped by a utilitarian seat, also built for durability. There is a seawater flushing valve, which allows the bowl to be filled with a suitable quantity of water, and rinsed when needed. At at the bottom of the bowl is a simple ball valve, controlled by a handle alongside the bowl. Use is easy: partially fill the bowl with seawater. Let nature take its course. And when all is done, pull the handle, thereby opening the ball valve and allowing the contents to flow via gravity down into a collection and holding tank (CHT) which other toilets also drain to. This CHT has a large valve through the hull, which connects directly to the sea. And it is also fitted with low-pressure compressed air lines.

Now, this is where the danger kicks in. From time to time, the CHT must be emptied. So a crewman called the Auxiliaryman of the Watch Forward goes around making sure that each and every ball valve is completely closed, and he hangs a warning sign on each toilet, advising that the head is secured while blowing sanitary systems. Once all is prepared, the CHT tank is pressurized with compressed air until the tank and its unsavory contents are at a pressure <u>above</u> that of the surrounding ocean. At 1000 feet of water depth, this is about **460 pounds per square inch!** And the hull valve is opened, blowing the sewage out into the ocean and making the nearby fish deliriously happy for a brief period of effortless feeding.

Care must be taken to avoid overblowing the tank, thereby releasing an air bubble into the sea which might betray the presence of the submarine. So typically, the tank is not completely emptied. The residual pressurized air now must be vented and the pressure relieved. This is done under control, via a series of charcoal air filters, but the entire boat is inevitably filled with the aroma of tank contents as the air flows back into the boat. This is not a popular aspect of submarine service, but it lasts for a relatively brief time before the air systems scrub away the offending odor.

And there is always a lurking chance of disaster. If the Auxiliaryman neglects to hang a warning sign, or if a crewman is in a hurry and simply thinks the process must be over by now and wants to ignore the sign, or fails to notice it, said crewman may do his business and open the toilet ball valve to the pressurized CHT. And physics takes over. A jet of liquefied waste under high pressure will come shooting up out of the toilet like Old Faithful geyser at Yellowstone National Park. I have heard of one officer who experienced this, was found covered in effluent, and when examined in sickbay had to have "material" flushed from beneath his eyelids. The overhead of the toilet compartment had to be completely scrubbed to clean it.

The next time you flush your toilet at home, consider what life might be like if it had the potential to do that to you.

CHAPTER 43

Overheard VHF

One of the eeriest things that ever happened to me at sea is a very vivid memory. One night in 1987, I was standing watch as Officer of the Deck (OOD) of my Guided Missile Frigate, operating off our home port of San Diego, California. It was a midwatch, well after midnight, and midwatches are usually quiet and fairly uneventful. Suddenly, our bridge-to-bridge radio squawked to life.

"Merchant vessel off my port bow, this is a US Navy warship on your starboard bow. What are your intentions, over?"

And I recognized the voice of an old friend. When I made my First Class Midshipman's cruise, I was assigned to USS *McINERNEY* (FFG-8), a guided missile frigate of the same class as my ship and homeported in Mayport, Florida. During a First

Class cruise, a Midshipman wears officer-like uniforms, is berthed in officer's country aboard the ship, and performs the duties of a junior officer, to help prepare him to be the junior officer he will soon enough become upon his commissioning. My supervisor and mentor during this cruise was a then-Lieutenant (O-3) named Leo, called Lee.

I was somewhat in awe of Lee, who was the Operations Officer and Navigator of *McINERNEY*. He was an excellent Surface Warfare Officer, skilled at his trade. He was an outstanding leader, liked and respected by his men. And he was a department head of a line warship and A FULL LIEUTENANT, which at the time seemed to me an exalted rank, far above that of a lowly First Class midshipman like me. I learned a great deal from Lee during that cruise, both about seamanship and about leadership. I had not seen him since 1981, but I had heard that he had been assigned as a Department Head aboard a large west-coast amphibious ship.

Flash forward six years, and I now held the same job, on a ship of the same class, as Lee had had when I knew him. I hoped that I was doing as well as he had done. Lee had a distinctive voice, and there was no doubt that it was he I was hearing on the radio that night.

"Merchant vessel off my port bow, this is a US Navy warship on your starboard bow. I am on course 030, speed 10 knots. What are your intentions, over?"

I heard no reply to Lee's query, but recognized that he must be standing watch as OOD aboard his ship, and that he must be concerned about a merchant vessel steaming near enough to his ship to pose a risk of collision. Colliding a Navy ship with any other vessel is one of the unpardonable sins of sea service. Nothing good comes from a collision, ever. (Web search "USS FITZGERALD incident" or "USS JOHN S. McCAIN incident" if you do not remember these recent examples of rank incompetence at sea. Neither is a pretty story.) Collision is a sure career killer for a Captain and for an OOD. And lives can be lost, quite easily.

Lee continued a series of increasingly-urgent radio calls, trying to get the merchant to answer him and to change course to avoid collision. Merchant ships are typically manned by small crews, and it is not unheard of for a foreign merchant ship to put the helm on autopilot, and for a lone bridge watchstander to leave the bridge to attend a call of nature, or get some coffee, or catch some sleep, or to otherwise be derelict in his duty, in direct violation of international law. It is illegal as hell, but it happens. And it was apparent to me that Lee's career and safety were diminishing by the moment as the merchant of concern was not responding.

Finally there was one last, urgent call: *"MERCHANT VESSEL OFF MY PORT BOW, THIS IS THE US NAVY WARSHIP. MY RUDDER IS RIGHT, MY ENGINES ARE BACK FULL."*

Lee was now maneuvering aggressively, obligated by the Rules of The Road to break his required maintenance of course and speed, to prevent an imminent collision. And I knew that Lee was aboard a large, ungainly amphibious ship with little agility and reserve power. Long moments of silence hung heavy as my friend's career hung in the balance.

Finally, Lee's obviously-relieved voice came over the radio. *"This is US Navy warship, resuming course 030, speed 10 knots."*

I breathed a long sigh of relief, as things had obviously worked out. A year or so later, I saw Lee in Hawaii, as both of our ships visited Pearl Harbor. He told me that he remembered the night in question, and that it had been a close call. The merchant ship never did respond, nor maneuver. What was also of great interest to me was that **the event had taken place over 100 miles from my ship, far beyond the normal range of the VHF bridge to bridge radio.** A condition called Tropospheric Ducting had trapped and reflected the radio signal to my ship, allowing me to hear a very distant half of a conversation with crystal clarity. The mystery and magic of radio had enabled me to listen in.

CHAPTER 44

Secure for Sea

One of the lessons sailors learn quickly is that their home upon the ocean is rarely if ever still. It moves in three dimensions, and when underway in any sort of weather at all, it moves A LOT. The smaller the ship, the more pronounced the motion. And just when you get used to the motion on any given day, any change in course, speed or weather and sea conditions changes the pattern of movement to something else. The disconnect between the inner ears' motion sensors and the eyes seeing the seemingly-fixed structure of the ship results in the violent nausea of seasickness. Believe me, I know a great deal about the *mal-de-mer* from personal experience.

If you are prone to it, it is an awful sensation, and it goes on for day after day. It can even be lethal if dehydration sets in because the sufferer cannot hold down any food or drink. And in the Navy, you still have to attend to your duties and stand your watches, seasickness or no.

Another aspect of all this movement is that anything that is not tied down or stowed in a proper rack or cabinet gets thrown around by the motion and gravity. If you know a sailor, you have probably noticed that they adhere pretty firmly to the motto of: "A place for everything and everything in its place." They have learned this lesson early and had it deeply ingrained in their daily routine, for good reason.

I remember an early object lesson in this imperative dictum of sea service. I was assigned to a guided missile cruiser for my first ship after I was commissioned. And unfortunately for me, that ship had just begun a year long shipyard overhaul. I wasn't going anywhere but to a drydocked hull for some time. But the USN still expected me and every other junior officer to learn our ship and our maritime trade, and to qualify as a Surface Warfare Officer in a reasonable amount of time. Imagine trying to learn how to fly a plane, drive a car or play golf simply by reading about it in books. You actually need to go to sea to learn how to be a sailor. So my ship arranged for me to go aboard a sister ship of a very similar class for a week or so, to help acclimate me to my new career. And I reported aboard USS HORNE (CG-30), with a crisp new seabag over my shoulder and shiny new gold Ensign's bars decorating my collar points. I was looking forward to seeing how a cruiser operated.

As I was not permanently assigned to the ship, they did not have an individual officer's stateroom vacant for me. In fact, there was only one bunk open in any officer's stateroom; that of the ship's Chaplain. This kind gentleman was a Lieutenant of the USN Chaplain's Corps, and as he occasionally needed a private space for counseling crew members, he had been assigned a two-man stateroom all to himself (until I came along and borrowed his upper bunk for a week.) He had gotten used to the stateroom being his personal space, and had filled it pretty full with various tools of his trade. We had to move a bunch of books, tracts, a guitar and other miscellany off of the bunk so that I could move into it. He graciously did this, but in a pretty haphazard fashion by my way of thinking. Still, I was an Ensign, he was a Lieutenant, and I kept my own counsel. The ship got underway from San Diego late in the afternoon, and I was assigned the midwatch (Midnight to 4:00 AM) as an observer on the bridge. After eating dinner in the wardroom, I decided it would be a good idea to get some rest before watch. So I hoisted myself up into the upper bunk, bid the Chaplain good night, and went to sleep.

After passing Point Loma and entering the Pacific, HORNE had initially set a comfortable course and speed en route to her designated operating area. Her motion was smooth and steady and not particularly vigorous. But within a couple of hours, she encountered the California Current, and the weather deteriorated somewhat. And once she got where she was going, she changed course and speed and set about her assigned operations. And her motion increased exponentially.

About 11:00 PM, I was awakened by a resounding bang. A whole shelf of the Chaplain's books came tumbling down onto the steel deck of the stateroom. Then a collection of religious tracts came fluttering down off of a cabinet top, flapping like crazed bats in a howling wind, then sliding to and fro as the ship rolled madly. Out of his bunk sprang the Chaplain, resplendent in only his underwear, as he tried to scoop up all the materials and restow them. Then his guitar crashed down, with a cacophonous jangling of its strings in protest. And on hands and knees, fighting for balance and purchase, he chased after all this stuff as his somehow now-unrestrained roller desk chair chased him back and forth across the stateroom on its casters. It was all I could do to keep from bursting out into laughter, as it was such a comical sight from my safe vantage point in the upper bunk. (I knew better than to offend a Lieutenant, and a holy man at that! Nothing good could come of that indiscretion. But who knew that Chaplains knew those particular sailor words?) I stayed out of his way and let him get on with the business of securing his stateroom for sea, about six hours too late. And I never forgot the lesson. "Secure for sea."

CHAPTER 45

UNREP and Breakaway Songs

One of the greatest strengths of the US Navy is its ability to replenish its ships while underway, in the battle area, rather than having to return to a port facility. This process allows refueling, restocking with needed stores, supplies and ammunition, and replacement of personnel, all while remaining at sea and on the move. When necessary, it can be done in conditions of complete radio silence, at night and in bad weather. These skills are not common to every navy in the world, and have been developed to their highest degree of expertise by our fleet.

An UNREP Fueling Station

So how do ships conduct Underway Replenishment, also known as UNREP? It is a complex dance of equipment and personnel, requiring tremendous skill. Enormous forces are at play, and it is inherently risky in several ways. But the USN does it routinely, maintaining this vital capability to an extremely high degree of combat readiness.

Let's assume that you are the Officer of the Deck of a destroyer. It has been about a week since your last replenishment, and you have been operating continuously all that time. Your Supply Officer drew up a list of needed support items and transmitted it via an encrypted radio message to the supply ship supporting your battle group a couple of days ago. This list included several thousand gallons of your main propulsion fuel, 100 gallons of diesel fuel, and about five hundred gallons of aviation fuel for your embarked helicopter. Additionally, you need to replenish the dry, fresh and frozen foodstuffs being consumed by your crew, and bring aboard some needed spare parts, consumable supplies and of course, a major morale item: postal mail! (Think of your weekly grocery run, but for a crew of about 330, living and working aboard a technologically-complex ship.) If your ship has been engaged in combat, you might also need to replenish the missiles and gun ammunition which you have fired. All of this has been requested and the support ship has pulled your order, prepared it for transfer and made ready to pass it to you this morning.

Your ship proceeded to an agreed-upon rendezvous position in the middle of the ocean. There you met up with the replenishment ship. They have set a course and speed which serve both the tactical situation and the weather conditions, so that the roll and pitch of the ship is minimized. You line your ship up behind them at about 600 yards and slightly to one side of their wake, while final preparations are made, matching their course and speed and holding station. They signal that they are preparing to receive you along their starboard side; they are already replenishing another ship of your battle group from their port side! Soon it will be your turn to commence. They hoist signal flag "Romeo" (the letter R) from a starboard halyard, but only about halfway up, or "at the dip." You answer by hoisting Romeo at the dip on your port side, indicating that you are preparing to come alongside. When she is ready for you, she will "close up" Romeo, or haul it all the way up. And when you commence your approach alongside her, your ship will also close up Romeo to full hoist. You then ring up more speed, so that you accelerate your 9000-ton ship to overtake the supply ship, advancing alongside her , and fighting the venturi suction created by the water passing through the gap between your hulls. When the timing is just right, you reduce your ordered speed to match the support's ship's (probably about 12-14 knots.) If you do this just perfectly, you glide into an exact position beside her, so that your replenishment stations align. Your two ships are now about 160 FEET apart. If you get too close, you collide. If you get too far apart, you can break the replenishment rig. You need to stay in this position, as closely as you can. This is akin to precision flying, but in ships weighing many thousands of tons. It requires skill to do this, and you have to maintain this position for an hour or two, in all weather up to Sea State 5 (8-12 foot seas, characterized as "very rough.") And oh, yes, you sometimes have to do this in the dark.

Unrep is pretty much an "all-hands-on-deck" evolution, with everyone topside dressed in life preservers, protective clothing and colored safety helmets denoting each man's job for easy identification. Everyone needed is stationed and standing by. The announcement is made over the loudspeaker: "Standby for shotlines, fore and aft." And at each end of the ship, a crewman fires a rifle loaded with a blank cartridge which launches a rubber plug attached to a very light nylon line across to the other ship. The line is taken in hand, and used to pull over a heavier messenger line, and then a "phone and distance line" which is passed to the bridge wing. This line is marked with numbered and colored flags and chemlights every twenty feet, so it becomes easy to monitor how far apart the ships are at any moment. It also provides sound-powered telephone voice contact between the two ships' bridges.

The messenger line is then used by the deck crewmen to pull over heavy steel cables which are attached to your ship above each replenishment station, and then tensioned using enormous hydraulic rams with cable pulleys which try to maintain a constant tension. One of these is rigged at each end of your ship. You are now tethered together with your support ship, fore and aft, by tensioned steel cables. And you maintain your position alongside, using constant rudder and speed corrections to do so. (Yes, this is as much art as science. Some officers drive better than others. It is a mark of seamanship.)

Perhaps your forward station is rigged to receive fuel. A large hose is sent over from the supply ship, with a special nozzle attached which fits into a matching receiver on your ship. Your crew pulls it across using its messenger line and latches it into place in the receiver. That receiver is ported through piping and valves, and aligned with the specific empty fuel tanks aboard your ship where you need THAT KIND of fuel to go. A separate hose brings a different kind of fuel to another fitting and alignment. And when all is ready, the support ship starts pumping fuel, at high rates of transfer.

Meanwhile, your after station is set up to receive dry cargo, which is contained in large cardboard containers called Tri-walls, suspended from heavy nylon cargo nets. Over the huge and heavy Tri-walls come; they are pulled across the intervening seas, are suspended over your deck and then lowered to it. As quickly as possible, the contents are manhandled into the ship for stowage in whatever place is appropriate. Here comes another Tri-wall. Repeat. And another. Repeat. All the while, both ships are underway, at night in 12-foot seas and howling winds. Can you see how this might be a bit dangerous?

If passengers need to be exchanged, they climb into a special chair and are passed along the wire between the ships, hopefully without suffering a dunking in the high seas as they transit the gap. Oh, I forgot to mention. Supply helicopters are also passing ammunition to you, by suspending it in nets beneath them, and easing it down onto your flight deck all the way aft, while the rest of the operation continues. It likewise must be safely handled and stowed in the proper magazines aboard the ship. Can you say "ballet, conducted by a cast of hundreds, on a hazardous, moving stage?"

When all is completed, the cargo nets and empty tri-walls retrograded back, and you have taken aboard another week's worth of the sinews of war, preparations are made to retrieve all the lines, wires and hoses, finally leaving only one wire attached. Upon signal, the final connection is severed by a quick release, and the wire is quickly spooled back aboard the replenishment ship. Your ship rings up power to accelerate away, and gently diverges in course so that you don't collide.

Here is where panache takes over. An old tradition among USN ships is that you want to look sporty as you part company. You drive smartly, speed away and play a unique tune called your "Breakaway Song" over your topside loudspeakers so that it is audible to the supply ships crew. Your song reflects your ship's unique personality (and perhaps your Captain's musical tastes.) In my ships, our breakaway songs at one time or another included *"On The Road Again"* by Willie Nelson, *"Long Train Runnin'"* by the Doobie Brothers, *"Home Sweet Home"* by Motley Crue, *"Break On Through To The Other Side"* by The Doors and *"Enter Sandman"* by Metallica. We actually once paraded a live band playing instruments on a high deck topside for extra style points! (They weren't that good, but made up in enthusiasm what they lacked in musical skill.)

Meanwhile, another ship is lined up aft, awaiting its turn to come alongside. Just another day at sea.

All hail the US Navy. This evolution is the pinnacle of the seaman's art, in my opinion. The next time you meet a qualified Surface Warfare Officer, spare a thought to his professional abilities, unsung though they usually are.

CHAPTER 46

Deperming

One of the more unique, albeit infrequent evolutions that a ship must undergo is called "Deperming." Ever since man realized that a metal object disturbs the earth's magnetic field (and some time afterward determined that this was a dandy way to get a torpedo or mine to explode near a ship without having to make physical contact with it), taking steps to minimize that metal ship's own magnetic field has been considered important. Deperming is that process; reducing to the maximum extent possible the ship's permanent magnetic signature.

When the ship was built, it was in a building dock aligned at a certain angle with the local magnetic field. The process of welding everything together permanently induced a magnetic field onto the ship itself. It is this field that we want to minimize. So after major structural work is done, a ship travels to a purpose-built facility called a Deperming Crib. The ship moors in the Crib. The crew then takes hold of messenger cables on both sides of the ship and uses them to pull large electrical cables which were resting on the bottom of the harbor onto and over the ship. This results in the ship being wrapped in dozens of slimy, muddy cables like being wound in a cocoon. Sensitive electronics have to be protected. And when all is ready, the cables are energized with a very high-voltage electrical current. This turns the ship into a huge electromagnet and permanently realigns its magnetic field to minimum configuration. (A separate Degaussing System built into the ship further reduces this signature when the ship operates day-to-day.)

I got a humorous exposure to the process of Deperming on my First Class Midshipman's Cruise aboard USS McINERNEY (FFG-8) in 1981. The ship had recently had some work done, so was ordered to deperm, and transited to Norfolk, Virginia where a Deperming Facility is located. We pulled in and before long, were treading gingerly over, under and around muddy, slimy, barnacle-encrusted cables fresh off the bottom of the Elizabeth River. The ship was a filthy shambles topside.

Just then, the telephone rang. It was Commander, Naval Surface Forces Atlantic (SURFLANT) calling. (My Captain's bosses' bosses' boss – a three-star admiral. Well, okay, it wasn't actually the Admiral on the phone, it was one of his underlings.) The situation was this. USS McINERNEY was the second ship of what eventually became a large class of guided missile frigates. But she was the shiny new frigate on the block. And the US Navy was hoping to market the ship's design to a number of other allied navies, including the perennially well-heeled Kingdom of Saudi Arabia. A delegation of Saudi naval officers happened to be visiting Norfolk that day, and SURFLANT "wondered if it would be convenient for them to visit McINERNEY – right now, today." And this wasn't a request.

So of course, amidst all the work, the ship had to plan a semi-diplomatic VIP visit. The Chief Petty Officer in charge of the Officer's Wardroom mess pulled together a quick set of refreshments and hors d'oeuvres to be served in the Wardroom. (This polite Filipino gentleman initially planned to present "a nice ham", but the ship's Supply Officer caught wind in time to have this religious faux pas avoided and shrimp cocktail was served instead.) And in about half an hour, here came a small boat with the Saudi delegation embarked. **They were wearing dress white uniforms and shoes.**

We ushered the officers aboard with due traditional ceremonies, and set about showing them the ship. It was hysterical, watching them try to avoid touching ANYTHING as they were shown the various corners of the ship, attempting to keep their pristine uniforms clean. And it became pretty apparent that the Saudis weren't particularly interested in the ship. They had plenty of money to afford any of a dozen larger, more capable and more expensive ships if they wanted them. They were simply humoring the USN's request that they give the ship and class a look and consideration. They didn't want to be there, and we didn't want to have them there! They came, they saw, they ate shrimp and they departed dirtier than they arrived. Diplomacy had been served. And then we got on with the business of deperming.

Surface Warfare Insignias – Enlisted Silver, Officer Gold

Submarine Warfare Insignias – Enlisted Silver, Officer Gold

CHAPTER 47

Qual Boards

The Navy is a skill-intensive profession by nature. In an environment that is always trying to kill you, aboard an extremely technically-complex machine that is a modern warship, there are many tasks that simply require expert execution. Even seemingly simple things can have serious consequences if done improperly. And some tasks can result in deaths, serious injuries and major damage if screwed up. So how does the Navy determine if a person has learned a task well enough to be allowed to perform it without supervision? In all cases, the Captain of the ship officially certifies that the sailor is qualified. And if the man later does something improperly that results in damage or disaster, the CAPTAIN is also held responsible, for he qualified the offending sailor. No Captain avoids the ultimately responsibility for anything that goes awry aboard his ship (unless the seemingly irresistible forces of 21st Century political correctness deem it in the Navy's progressive interest that blame be affixed elsewhere. (See the *USS FITZGERALD* incident, look closely at who was involved and on watch in CIC, and read between the lines.) No matter that those same forces may have pressured the Captain to deem someone qualified even if he had misgivings. But that is another story for another day.)

A Navy Junior Officer is assigned to a ship first and foremost to lead a division of sailors. But the JO is also expected to learn his trade, in part by qualifying in and performing specific watchstanding duties. Among these are:

- Officer of the Deck (In-port). This is the person responsible for controlling access to the ship, and overseeing the evolutions, daily routine and general communications of the ship when in port. He conducts honors and ceremonies as required. He stands his watch on the Quarterdeck.

- Command Duty Officer: The senior officer in charge of a duty section in port. When everyone else goes home, this officer is in full charge of the ship in the Captain's absence. I once had to get my ship underway as CDO, WITHOUT THE CAPTAIN ABOARD. This is not usual.

- Conning Officer: the person who gives orders to the Helmsman, directing the movement of the ship in all underway evolutions.

- Junior Officer of the Deck (Underway.) This person assists the Officer of the Deck in supervising and directing all aspects of the Ship's operations when underway.

- Combat Information Center Watch Officer. This officer supervises the ship's Combat Information Center, where the electronic sensors and weapons are controlled and a duplicate navigation plot maintained.

- Engineering Officer of the Watch: the person who supervises the operation of the ship's main propulsion, electrical power generation, and auxiliary systems machinery. This is an extremely complex engineering plant, akin to the infrastructure that supports a small town.

- And most importantly, Officer of the Deck (Underway). This is the officer who is responsible for all aspects of a ship's operations when underway, including its safe navigation and maneuvering.

- When an officer has learned a comprehensive understanding of his ship, it's systems and general shipboard operations and engineering, he is deemed qualified as a Surface Warfare Officer (or Submarine Officer, with its unique requirements and watch stations achieved along the way), and is entitled to wear that insignia for the rest of his career.

- And in time, it must be determined that an officer is actually qualified to assume and be given command of a ship. This is, naturally, called Command Qualification. It is typically earned at career midpoint, about 8-12 years into a 20+year career.

A time-honored rite of passage and system of ensuring that an officer is in fact competent in the major tasks that he must master is the Qualification Board. When the Officer has completed all the paperwork, and stood the watch successfully under supervision for some time such that his chain of command thinks he is ready, he is called before a Qual Board for the watch station in question. This board is comprised of several individuals who are themselves qualified and have long experience in the task. It almost always includes a senior officer and may include the Captain himself, or not. It's his call, as it is ultimately his responsibility.

The officer presents his written record of task qualification for review, if any. He is then questioned by the members of the board, at length, to test his knowledge of the task. This can be highly technical in nature. I remember one question asked of me at my Surface Warfare Officer qual board: "You are a molecule of water in the main condenser. Describe your passage through the ship's main propulsion system's major components, giving your state, temperature and pressure at each step along the way."

Questions might also be situational: " You are underway, transiting San Diego harbor en route to sea. You are on channel course, at speed 10 knots. Just as you are abeam Shelter Island in mid-channel, you lose main steering control of the ship's rudder. What do you do?" This tests not only the officer's knowledge of the steering equipment, but also his grasp of procedures, his judgment and ability to think quickly.

Another possible question: "Describe the process of mooring the ship to the pier. What are your likely rudder and engine commands, what mooring lines are used, and how might you use them to get the ship in proper position alongside?"

And another: "A fire breaks out in the Main Engine Room. A leaking flange is spraying atomized lubricating oil onto hot equipment and it has flashed into a fire. What do you do and what happens now?"

And another: "Describe the ship's weapons systems, from longest to shortest range. What are the capabilities of each system and how many of them do we carry at full load? "

And if the officer knows as much as he should, answers well and keeps his composure, the Board reports him ready, the Captain signs a qualification letter, and he begins to stand that watch or is granted that permanent qualification. And before he knows it, he is sitting on the other side of the table, as a member of a qual board examining a more junior officer.

CHAPTER 48

Launching, Commissioning and Decommissioning

It is hard for a landsman to comprehend the bond sailors develop with their ships. It is often a deep, lifelong affair, an abiding affection which transcends time and distance. Your ship is your home for a time. She conveys you to faraway lands, and is the scene of unforgettable experiences. As Oliver Wendell Holmes once famously wrote, *"In our youth, our hearts were touched with fire."* Even a peacetime sailor has seen his share of risks aboard his ship. Her hull is your shelter. She provides your food, your water and your heat or cooling. The strength of her hull and the power of her engines are all that stand between you and the incredible power of a hungry ocean. You stand watch upon countless watch, hour upon tedious hour upon her decks, and you learn her unique sounds, motions and ways. Your time aboard her is but one tiny part of a much longer continuum of service, shared by generations of crew members across several decades. And in time of war or disaster, she will either see you safely through, or become the site of your burial service, or perhaps even serve as your eternal tomb.

Ships are living, breathing things, more than the sum of the human lives aboard them. They have individual personalities; true, the Captain's own personality has a lot to do with the character of a particular ship's nature, but not everything. Other key crew members put their mark upon her as well. Ships can be happy, or unhappy. They can be lucky, or decidedly unlucky, to the point of being considered jinxed. Sailors are a superstitious lot, and have been for millennia, probably because human experience has noted this phenomenon repeatedly across the eons. So sailors have long understood this reality, and deeply ingrained traditions have formed in recognition of it. The ceremonies attendant to bringing a ship to life, and ultimately laying it to rest are excellent examples of these traditions.

Keel Laying: A ship begins its life when its central structural member, its keel, is laid down in the building dock. Modern ships are often built in sections which are assembled in order and later welded together, but the central lower strength girder is her keel and the first one gets laid somewhere. That is usually marked by a ceremony. It is akin to the egg being fertilized in the womb, and the very first spark of life flickering into existence. I know of one important ship which serves our Navy today, *USS ARLEIGH BURKE* (DDG-51). She is the lead ship of the finest class of destroyers which has ever gone to sea, and was named for a famed World War II hero, later an Admiral and the Chief of Naval Operations. Read his biography if you want to see what a fighting sailor can look like. In only the fourth event of its type since the civil war, *USS ARLEIGH BURKE* was named for Admiral Burke **while he was still alive**, and he was present at her commissioning on the 4th of July, 1991. But well before that, he welded his signature onto her keel at her keel laying ceremony. It remains there today.

Another ancient practice was the placing of a silver coin below the base of the central mast of a ship, as an offering to the gods for luck, or should she sink, as payment for the souls aboard her's passage across the River Styx and into the underworld. In ancient greek mythology, Charon the Ferryman would not transport the soul of anyone across the black river without payment, and they would wander the far riverbank for eternity. This is why corpses were buried with coins (an *obolus* in latin) upon their eyes; as fare payment for the departed soul. And some ships even today have a silver coin placed below their mast when it is erected, where it remains for the life of the ship. (As a personal note, there is a silver coin beneath the mast of my small sailboat. I cover all my bases...)

Launching/Christening: When the ship under construction is ready enough, she must be moved from her building dock into the water. Ships are built on the land, but are built for the sea. And while she will on occasion be drydocked again, this is the very first time she will touch the water that is her natural element and where she will spend the preponderance of her life. The Launching Ceremony is akin to a human being born, and entering the world it will ever after inhabit. In our Christian society, the ship is usually formally christened, and given her official name, before God and an assembled group of witnesses, with prayers for her safety and that of all the souls who will sail in her. She is decorated with flags and bunting. The ship's sponsor (almost invariably a woman, usually a political appointment, someone with money or association with the ship's history, namesake or building yard) stands on a platform beside the ship's bow with a bottle of champagne suspended on a rope. At the key moment, she pronounces the ship's name and smashes the bottle on the bow, where the bubbling spirit wets the hull (this is in fact an ancient historical echo of the pagan practice of offering a libation sacrifice to the gods while asking for their protection and benevolence towards the ship.) The keel blocks are struck away, and the vessel down slides into the water on rails with a resounding splash, and (hopefully) bobs there proudly and upright. (Traditionally, this motion was backwards, with her stern entering the water first, followed by the bow. But in modern yards, ships are sometimes launched sideways. Browser search "ship launching" for some interesting videos.)

Commissioning: Construction continues, and eventually, the ship is completed, sea trialed and accepted by the Navy from its builders. It is time to bring the ship into active service, placing her "in commission." This impressive ceremony marks the beginning of her active career as a warship. Guests are seated on the pier and the ship's crew is paraded in ranks behind them. Everyone is in dress uniform and festive bunting marks this as a special occasion. Speeches are made, the Captain is formally presented with the ship and ordered to bring it to life.

Up to this point, the ship has been sitting lifeless, motionless, There are no flags flying, and no one visible aboard. When the order is given, at first, nothing changes. Then the ship speaks, for the first time. Her whistle lets out a long, piercing blast. High atop the mast, a radar begins to turn. Then another. Then her gun mounts and missile launchers begin to move, as if seeking an enemy. Flags are hoisted aloft, and full-dress signal flags start to rise above her deck and flutter in the breeze. The ship transforms from a dead, cold thing to a moving, living thing, before the eyes of the assembled guests. And the crew runs aboard to man the rails, taking their places as the original members of what will over the next several decades be many crews. Historically, ships had teak wood decks, and each crew member would receive a piece of wood left over from construction as a memento of his service in that first, original crew. Such original crewmembers are still called "plankowners."

Decommissioning: After many intervening decades of service, a ship is determined to no longer be technologically relevant. Her hull and engines are tired, her structure battered by sea service, and her weapons systems and sensors are far behind the state of the art. It is time to retire her as an active warship, or to take her "out of commission." The last crew ever to serve the ship has spent many months preparing her for this day. All weapons are removed, she is defueled and her stores are taken ashore. All flammables are removed, and all accountable equipment inventoried and turned in for re-issuance to another ship if needed. Everything else is removed, and in many cases simply trashed. Some items are presented to crew members as mementos; I know the last Chaplain assigned to USS CHARLES F. ADAMS (DDG-2), who is an ordained Episcopal priest. Ships with assigned chaplains have a standard-issue portable field communion set. It contains everything a minister needs to administer the sacrament of holy communion or last rites, in an OD green nylon satchel which can be easily transported to wherever the padre needs to hold that service. The ship had the bag embroidered with the ship's name and dates of service, and presented the communion set to my friend as his memento upon decommissioning. I once took communion from him from that historic Navy service.

Finally, on the appointed day, a ceremony is held formally retiring the ship, with assembled guests. Every living former Commanding Officer is invited to attend, and many do. Lots of former crewmembers likewise are invited and come from all over the USA to attend. And when the order is given, the ship's equipment is stilled, her crew marches from her deck onto the pier, and her flags, ensign and commission pennant are hauled down for the last time. And in a moment, she goes from being a living, breathing thing, a servant of our nation with a long record of duty, to a cold and lifeless hunk of steel. She will never again move under her own power.

So what happens to ships when they are decommissioned? Some are kept in a state of preservation (informally called "being mothballed") so they can be reactivated if needed in a national emergency. Others are given or sold to allied navies who can still get some use out of them. One of my former ships continues to serve in the Turkish Navy. A few are taken to sea and used as targets, sunk by weapons fire from younger siblings, thereby performing one final service by training a new generation of fighting sailors or testing new generations of weapons. A very few are intentionally sunk as scuba diving attractions or artificial reefs. But most are ignominiously sold for recycling of their materials , auctioned off and broken up as scrap metal. To my way of thinking this is the worst possible fate. The noble old girl served our country for decades,standing her watch of deterrence and perhaps getting in a few licks against our enemies. She carried many generations of sailors across countless ocean miles. She earned honorable retirement. And one day, she is hauled up on shore, cut into pieces and hauled away to a smelter. Nothing remains but the pride which her crew will always have in her when her name is mentioned. But a lucky few will live again; the USN likes to recycle ship names, so in time a new warship may be given the name and start the process all over again.

CHAPTER 49

Divine Services

The Church Pennant

Historically, the Navy has done its best to support the spiritual needs of its sailors assigned to fleet units. Larger ships in the Navy often have an ordained minister assigned to them, who is commissioned as an officer of the USN Chaplain Corps. My first ship had one. These maritime men of the cloth hold divine services, act as spiritual counselors and generally look to the welfare of the crew. When needed, they can also perform baptisms, last rites, burial services and if ordained in a faith that requires it, confessors. If a ship does not have its own Chaplain, one may visit from time to time when the ship is deployed to hold worship services and provide holy communion to crew members who desire to attend. There is also an enlisted rating, the Religious Programs Specialist (RP). These sailors assist Chaplains in conducting their duties in support of the fleet. It is not at all uncommon for a helicopter to bring a Chaplain and an RP aboard on a Sunday when deployed. They visit, set up and conduct a service, and then are whisked away to repeat the process on another ship.

When the ship is actually conducting a divine worship service, there is a special pennant (The Church Pennant) flown. It is unique in design and is the only pennant ever flown above the National Ensign (Old Glory, our nation's flag. And the word is passed over the General Announcing System : *"Divine services are being held in (name of space.) Knock off all games and unnecessary work. Maintain quiet about the decks during divine services."*

An interesting digression: if a sailor wishes to have his child baptized or christened aboard his ship, the Chaplain can make it happen. According to tradition, the ship's bell is inverted and filled with baptismal water, and the sacrament is performed over and in the bell, using it as the baptismal font. And the child's name is engraved inside the bell, where it remains forever.

Chaplains can perform weddings aboard ship, I suppose. I have never heard of it being done, but in the Navy of the 21st Century, nothing would surprise me.

In combat, you can be sure that the Chaplain would be about the decks, leading prayer, offering comfort and attending to the wounded and dying. US Navy history is replete with examples of courage and heroism by its Chaplains. A couple of events especially stand out.

"Sudden death was everywhere. . ."

On the morning of March 19, 1945, about fifty miles off the coast of Japan, the aircraft carrier USS Franklin was bombed by Japanese aircraft. Two heavy bombs penetrated the hangar deck killing everyone inside. The planes on the flight deck were knocked into the air, their whirling propellers smashing gas tanks which spilled 17,000 gallons of gasoline. Fires raged from stem to stern on three decks. For four interminable hours, explosions rocked the Franklin. All communications, fire mains and power were gone. Into the thick of the choking smoke and fury came a hero with a white cross on his helmet. "Padre" to the Catholic, "Rabbi Joe" to the Jewish boys, Chaplain Joseph Timothy O'Callahan was "Father" to everyone on board. He was seemingly everywhere, performing last rites, leading prayer, offering encouragement and demonstrating leadership of the highest order.

When the Franklin finally limped into Pearl Harbor, it was the most damaged ship ever to reach port. Its casualty list was the highest in Navy history--432 dead and over 1,000 wounded. "Big Ben" was bombed, battered, bruised and bent, but like the spirit of the men on board, she was not broken.

For his conspicuous gallantry above and beyond the call of duty, Father Joseph T. O'Callahan received the only Congressional Medal of Honor ever awarded a Navy chaplain."

And another:

George Snavely Rentz was born on July 25, 1882 in Lebanon Pennsylvania. He attended and graduated from Princeton Theological Seminary. Following his ordination by the Presbytery of Northumberland in 1909, he preached to churches across Pennsylvania and New Jersey for eight years. He was appointed acting chaplain with the rank of Lieutenant Junior Grade and assigned to the 11th regiment of Marines in France shortly following entry of the United States into World War I. He attained the rank of Commander in 1924; among his sea duty assignments he served onboard USS Florida (BB-30),USS Wright (AV-1),USS West Virginia (BB-48), and USS Augusta (CA-31). In 1940, when the USS Houston (CA-30) relieved Augusta as flagship of the Asiatic fleet extended his tour in the region as ships company on the USS Houston. It was aboard this cruiser he served so devotedly and enthusiastically, providing the ship's crew and officers with great hope and promise.

During an allied attack on February 4, 1942, Houston was under severe air attack. Commander Rentz spurned cover and circulated among the crew of the anti-aircraft battery, encouraging them. One officer noted, "when the sailors saw this man of God walking fearlessly among them, they no longer felt alone." The Houston took a direct hit during the attack that disabled Turret III and killed 48 men. A month later, Houston engaged in the Battle of the Java Sea alongside the Australian light cruiser HMAS Perth. Both ships were outnumbered by a Japanese troop convoy but they persisted in the ensuing melee of fire. The USS Houston fought valiantly throughout the violent meeting but eventually succumbed to a barrage of torpedo fire and began to sink into The Pacific. The crew clung to floating wreckage as they were forced to abandon the ship. Chaplain Rentz and several others found themselves on a pontoon that was fast taking on water. Chaplain Rentz made several attempts to give up his life jacket to the young sailors on the wreckage. Having felt that he had lived his life to the fullest and according to God's will, he removed his jacket, handed it to a seaman and said a quick prayer and then swam away from the group on the pontoon on the morning of March 1, 1942. This selfless act of heroism resulted in Chaplain Rentz being the only Navy chaplain to be awarded the Navy Cross, the United States Navy's second highest award for valor.

Chaplains also conduct the solemn service of Burial At Sea. The Sailor's body is placed in a wrapping shroud, with weight added to ensure that it sinks rapidly. Historically, this was the sailor's hammock (his bed) but the navy no longer uses hammocks.

Burial At Sea

If this is a planned funeral vice a combat loss, the body may be in a standard casket, but one which has been drilled so that it will flood and sink. The body is placed on a wide board, usually a tabletop, and covered with the flag. The Chaplain reads the service and offers prayers, finally uttering the phrase "we commit his body to the deep." The bugle call " Taps" is played, rifle volleys are fired, and the end of the board lifted, allowing the body to slide over the side and into the water which will be the sailor's eternal grave.

In the event that a veteran has requested burial at sea, it is also performed by a fleet unit when operations allow. Usually this is a scattering of cremated ashes over the stern, with accompanying service performed by a Chaplain.

CHAPTER 50

The Worst Jobs Aboard Ship

I'm sure that I have mentioned before that there are a lot of uncomfortable aspects to shipboard naval service. Hazards abound, and they will be the subject of another tale. But as in any home, or business, or city, there are a few "dirty jobs" which no one really WANTS to do, but someone HAS to do. These tasks are usually farmed out to the most junior sailors, or to someone who has incurred his Chief Petty Officer's displeasure by dint of some wrongdoing or other. I will relate a few of these unpleasant jobs. And remember, all of these take place aboard a moving, rolling ship (or submarine), often thousands of miles from home, after months of separation from loved ones and "normal" life, and under a near-constant condition of sleep deprivation. Sometimes being a sailor just ain't much fun.

Heavy Weather Lookout: By international law, a ship must maintain a proper visual lookout topside, 24x7. That means three sailors (port, starboard and aft) must be outside, in the weather, at all times. Hot, cold, snowing, ice storm, dust storm, heavy seas, you name it. They are rotated to keep them healthy and alert, but when the weather is inclement, this is most uncomfortable. Not fun.

Scullery duty: The ship's galley feeds a crew of hundreds to perhaps thousands of sailors. "Three hots and a cot" (meaning three square meals a day and a place to sleep) are absolute guarantees of an enlistment contract for every sailor. And while trained and rated specialists prepare these meals relatively expertly, the less technically demanding tasks of washing dishes, grinding up and disposing of garbage, food scraps and packaging are performed on a rotating basis by junior enlisted men detailed to the Supply Department for the purpose. This is historically called "mess cooking" duty. Imagine working in the garbage grinder space, processing hundreds of pounds of food scraps, spoiled produce, potato peelings, rancid milk, etc. After every meal. Not fun.

Bilge Cleaning: Cleanliness is very important onboard ship. It is a matter of disease prevention, yes. Lots of sailors packed into a metal box can easily contract any number of infectious diseases if a high state of sanitation is not maintained. But in engineering and operations spaces, cleanliness is also about industrial safety. Engineering spaces are particularly difficult to keep clean. Oily deck plates are slip and trip hazards. Common dust, (the majority of which is shedded human skin flakes) is highly flammable. And a variety of flammable substances (fuel oil, lubricating oils and greases, hydraulic fluids, etc are contained in piping moving through the space. Pipe fittings, operating equipment and daily maintenance unavoidably allow some of these inherently hazardous substances to leak into the space, down through the gratings and deck plates and into the lowest recesses of the hull, called the bilges. There, they mix with or float on top of some quantity of seawater which finds its way into the bilges as well. Seawater is full of microscopic organic life forms; these die and decay, giving off odors. So from time to time, sailors have to loosen the deck plates and crawl down into the bilges to degrease, clean and wipe them down if necessary. This is a confined, uncomfortable area, with lots to bang your head, knees and elbows on. And the ship doesn't stop moving! Not fun.

Operating equipment: Occasionally, a particular piece of equipment may be a terrible taskmaster. I can think of two in my experience. One was a hydraulic accumulator, which served to pressurize and store hydraulic fluid in readiness to perform work in other connected equipment. This piece of equipment was placed far to one side of the engine room of a submarine, against the curved hull of the boat. There were several pipes running alongside the hull behind the unit. And the Accumulator leaked a bit. There was a constantly-forming puddle of hydraulic fluid which seeped out and around the base of the unit. I was assigned to keep this area clean on a daily basis. And in time, I found the only way to wipe up the hydraulic fluid behind the equipment foundation was to get another sailor to help me go in between the frames of the hull, behind the horizontal piping, headfirst. I would take along a wiping rag or three, and wipe up the oil while he held my ankles and helped pull me back out when I was done. Not fun.

The other beast was a large industrial document shredder, with huge, rotating, razor-sharp blades. My Radiomen had to destroy large quantities of printed message traffic, classified publications and used or canceled cryptographic material every week, using this shredder. It was mounted in a closet along a passageway, barely big enough to hold the unit and the operator with the door closed. It vibrated, roared, and generated huge quantities of dust and heat when in operation for a multi-hour shred session. The operator had to wear goggles, a dust mask, hearing protection and coveralls, and would sweat profusely in the confined space, emerging looking a bit like a sheep covered in white dust. It got so bad that one day, the equipment malfunctioned hugely and the operator shut it down immediately after starting. It became apparent that someone had dumped a handful of ball bearings into the hopper, sabotaging the machine and basically destroying it beyond repair. Document destruction was done in a burn barrel on the fantail for the rest of that deployment. We never did find out who had done the deed. Not fun x 2.

Head Cleaning: Of course, like any home or business, there are restroom facilities serving the occupants. These are shared, public rest rooms; think of a truck stop frequented by 150-200 sailors a day. Sailors come from all walks of life; some are more conscientious and cleaner in their habits than others. Some are seasick. Some may have intestinal illnesses. So the heads are less then pristine at any given moment other than just before an inspection. Someone has to clean them. Not fun.

Tank inspection: Speaking of the heads, some sailor has to maintain the equipment, like your civilian plumber. (On my first ship, a clog of the piping from one crew's head was discovered to be someone's dead baby rabbit. Heaven only knows how he got it aboard or why he flushed it instead of simply throwing it overboard.) But it is not normal for anyone to actually enter your septic tank. When a ship undergoes overhaul, the Collection, Holding and Transfer tanks which collect the sewage are cleaned and hydroblasted to keep them working well for another 3-5 years. And when that process is done, someone has to enter and inspect the tank to certify that it is properly done, and that no equipment, tools or other material which could clog the system are left inside. Not fun.

The Drain Pump Strainer: the worst job I personally ever had to do. On a submarine, all waste water as well as sewage must be collected so that it can be ejected from the boat under pressure, under control. So toilets drain to one tank (previously described in Chapter 42 *Submarine Toilets*.) But the sinks and showers drain "gray water" to a different set of tanks, which are then pumped into a main collection tank for disposal, via a very powerful Drain Pump. This Drain Pump is protected from ingesting too much foreign material which could clog or damage it by a large duplex strainer. This has a perforated steel / wire mesh basket which catches all the stuff you don't want to go into the pump, but which some sailor felt it was appropriate to let flow down the sink or shower drain. If you have daughters, you already know what a horror the bathroom sink drain is due to hair clogs. Add mucus, saliva and toothpaste residue. Perhaps hair gel. Multiply by a crew of 150 or so. Now, to put this delicately......a submarine shower is like a stainless steel telephone booth with a drain in the floor. It is completely enclosed and is THE ONLY PLACE ONBOARD THE BOAT WHERE AN ENLISTED MAN CAN FIND ANY PRIVACY. And some sailors, for reasons I do not understand, think it is appropriate to defecate in the shower and then smush it down the drain. Don't ask me; I'm just telling you what the Hull Technicians have told me. And oh yes, any other "secretions" created and then eliminated by sailors far from home find their way into the drain on very frequent occasions. And eventually, all of that finds its way to the drain pump strainer......which some poor sailor has to periodically open, and scrape clean with a steel implement, restoring the smooth flow of gray water. NOT FUN!

CHAPTER 51

Widow Makers

Working aboard a warship at sea is inherently hazardous. The ocean itself is dangerous. Heavy seas and hurricane winds can sink a ship and kill everyone aboard. Falling overboard can kill you from striking the sea from a great height (a large ship), by getting sucked into and chopped into hunks by the propellers (any ship) or simply by hypothermia or drowning. (In my day, many very large ships had one or two sailors go overboard on deployments; these are often suicides, and it is not uncommon to find the sailor's shoes and uniform folded by the rail from which he jumped. I would bet that the infrequent murder takes place like this as well. I suspect the statistics remain about the same today.) But aside from the ocean environment, there are plenty of other very dangerous elements within the lifelines which can kill you deader than hell. I call these "widow makers" and will list a few for your consideration.

The risks of the explosion of weapons, or fire caused by burning fuel or oil is pretty self-apparent. There are lots of weapons and flammable substances onboard ship. Enough said.

Aviation: Working on the flight deck of any air-capable ship is dangerous, day or night. Deck space is extremely limited and busy. Helicopters hovering generate large static electricity charges; touching the bird or any suspended load before grounding with a shorting probe can electrocute you. Spinning rotors are invisible and can behead you in the blink of an eye; the tail rotor is especially deadly. If a man forgets and gets too close to the tail (or the pilot loses control and the tail gets too close to the man), it's lights out. And on an Aircraft Carrier flight deck, jet engines can blow a sailor off the edge of the ship, or suck them into the jet engine. Night operations are extremely dangerous, what with all the noise, jet and rotor blast and confusion. It takes constant situational awareness to work there safely. Add in jet fuel and live explosive ordnance. It's a deadly playground.

Electricity: our great enabler, electricity makes our modern technological society possible. Normally, we harness it in dozens of ways each day without a second thought. But onboard ship, it can kill. If a piece of electrical equipment is properly grounded, no problem (usually). But if the grounding strap breaks, or is improperly installed, or gets painted over so that it becomes resistant rather than conductive, and a sailor touches the equipment, it can short to the ground of the steel deck VIA THE BODY of the sailor. **Bzzzzzt. KAPOW.** Dead sailor. Sometimes, ungrounded equipment can simply charge the steel deck. And if a sailor standing on the deck touches the overhead or another unconnected steel element, he finds himself right in the middle of what is essentially an electrical capacitor: a component which stores a large electrical charge and discharges it all at once when that charge's voltage exceeds the resistance of the dielectric, or resistive medium in the middle. **Bzzzzzt. KAPOW.** Dead sailor. I once saw a training aid of a gold wedding band welded to the shank of a large screwdriver. A sailor had been working with the screwdriver on a piece of energized equipment and contrary to good industrial safety practice, had left his wedding ring on his finger. Electricity did it's thing, welding the ring to the screwdriver and amputating the man's ring finger. Word was there was no bleeding, as the electrical burn instantly cauterized the stump.

Rotating machinery: Equipment spinning at high speed can crush, grab or amputate if a sailor gets caught in it. There are lots of pieces of equipment going roundy roundy in any ship, at all times. The most interesting one of these I ever heard about was told to me by a Machinery Repairman Chief Petty Officer assigned to my Division. He was kind enough to show me the basics of how to run a metal lathe, which was an impressive skill he had in spades. As a cautionary tale, he related the time as a junior sailor in his first machine shop when he saw a shipmate get killed before his eyes. The man chucked a long, thick piece of brass bar stock into a lathe, grossly off-center, and flipped on the lathe. Unfortunately, the lathe was set to high speed. It spun so fast that the centrifugal force imparted to the off-center brass bar spun it outward, easily bending the malleable brass and smashing it into the man's skull, splattering his brains all over the shop. Needless to say , I was very careful about lathe settings when I played with the equipment after that.

Steam: My first ship was steam powered, and every nuclear-powered ship in the Navy (every submarine, and aircraft carrier) is still steam powered. Steam must be placed at very high temperatures and pressures to contain enough energy to drive a multi-thousand ton ship. In my ship, that meant 1200 PSI and 950F. The steam system can develop a leak either through a flange fastener failing, a pinhole or crack developing at a hot spot caused by a corrosive deposit formed due to improper water chemistry in the system, or by shock caused by explosive attack (torpedo, bomb or missile.) Everyone can relate to a minor steam burn. You probably got one as a child "experimenting" with your mother's steam iron or cook pot. But main propulsion steam is another animal entirely. A superheated high pressure steam leak is clear and invisible. It can cut a man in two like an enormous claymore sword. When in engineering, if an unusual, extremely loud rushing sound starts up, you STAND STILL. Then someone grabs a broom and starts inching forward, waving it around until the broom head gets cut off or bursts into flame. That's how you find the leak. (A tip of the hat to steam engineers: I was always in awe of those guys, doing uncomfortable work in hot, humid spaces, far below decks, not knowing what was going on topside, just keeping the ship moving, the lights on and all the equipment running. The repetitive heat stress they endured aged them prematurely; most old "snipes" (as engineers are lovingly called by their shipmates) are actually younger than they look.)

Elevators and dumbwaiters: Large ships frequently have a need to move heavy things up or down between decks. This is accomplished using mechanical elevators and dumbwaiters. And every year or so, some sailor is killed when he starts up the elevator, doesn't see it appear when he expects to, and sticks his head into the shaft or trunk to look and see what the problem is. Chop. Crush. Dead sailor.

Torpedo Fuel: Torpedoes run on a special type of extremely noxious fuel. It is deadly, before and after it is burned in the torpedo's engine. The exhaust is especially toxic. If a torpedo happens to start running in the room before being locked into the torpedo tube, it can kill very quickly.

Toxic and explosive gas: The decomposition of organic material generates hazardous gases. In a confined space made of metal, there is no place for the gas to dissipate to, and it builds up and concentrates. Some of the biggies of concern aboard ship are methane, carbon monoxide and hydrogen sulfide. Any of these in sufficient concentration can render a sailor unconscious and kill them almost instantly. So particular care must be taken when entering a confined space which is not normally ventilated or occupied (like a tank or void space.) A man goes in wearing a breathing apparatus and a gas test should be performed. A retrieval line should also be attached. The last thing that should happen is a man goes in alone and unprotected, and drops. Another shipmate finds them, rushes in to "save them"...and drops. Repeat until someone does it right and retrieves the bodies.

Fate and Flying Objects: The strangest case of shipboard death I ever heard of in my career took place aboard an *OLIVER HAZARD PERRY*-class Guided Missile Frigate *USS ANTRIM* (FFG-20). It was February of 1983. The ship was fortunate to have a civilian teacher aboard. The Program for Afloat College Education (PACE) was a great way for sailors to learn and earn college credits while aboard ship in their spare time. An accredited educator would come aboard and deploy with the ship and hold classes. He got paid, got a sea adventure, and sailors got desired college education. Everybody won. Except this time. The ship was conducting a live weapons shoot of their PHALANX Close In Weapons System (CIWS) at a target drone simulating a sea-skimming cruise missile. The CIWS is a radar-guided six-barrel gatling gun, which fires 20mm depleted uranium shells at an astonishing rate of 3000 or 4500 rounds per minute (that's 50 or 75 rounds per SECOND.) As the CIWS was mounted aft on that class of ship, the drone approached from right aft and was flying close but parallel to the ship's track. The CIWS did its job well, and shot down the drone...which did an uncommanded leftward dive, plunged into the sea, skipped off the water and slammed into the side of the ship, killing the PACE instructor in his stateroom.

Going to sea isn't all mermaids, liberty ports and sunsets. Sometimes it can get you killed in creative ways.

CHAPTER 52

Navyisms

Sea Service has its own traditional language, some of which finds its antecedents in ancient history. So everyday things have unique nautical names. Sailors are also a creative bunch. Perhaps it's the boredom, or maybe it's because sea service can be so arduous that if you don't laugh, you may cry on occasion. For whatever reason, sailors often come up with some hilarious expressions or alternate names for common objects or situations.

Some unique names:

A ship is a Ship, never a "boat" (with the notable exception of submarines, which are ALWAYS "Boats", never ships. As a general rule, a Boat can fit on a Ship.

A stairway is never a stairway aboard ship, or ashore. It is a "Ladder."

The Smoking Lamp: Before the USN quite recently forbade tobacco use onboard ships, smoking was very common. In fact, when I began my Navy service, a non-smoker was more unusual than normal. By the time I left active duty, I was a member of a completely non-smoking wardroom. And when smoking was allowed to take place, The "Smoking Lamp" was deemed "Lit" and when smoking was forbidden (during refueling, for example) the Smoking Lamp was deemed "Out". This refers back to the days of sail. Sources of fire were strictly controlled on wooden ships with tarred natural cordage and gunpowder aboard. No man carried around a Zippo lighter and just blazed up whenever he felt like it. A special oil lamp was kept lit topside and a man took his tobacco to that one lantern to light it. And when lighting up was forbidden, the lamp was extinguished to prevent smoking.

When a disciplinary hearing or trial took place, whether a court martial or a non-judicial punishment hearing (called Captain's Mast, as it took place below decks at the ship's mast) the long wooden table where the Authority sat would traditionally be covered with a green baize tablecloth. Going to either is called "Facing the Long Green Tablecloth."

Flogging used to be a common punishment for misbehaviors, even fairly trivial ones. A particularly harsh punishment was reserved for the most heinous crimes short of hanging: "Flogging Around The Fleet" – where a man would be taken to each ship of the fleet, flogged, and then taken to the next. They often died before it was all over. Flogging was performed with a special cotton cord whip with nine braided strands, called "the Cat 'O Nine Tails." Lashes were rendered in sets of dozens. One, Two, Three Dozen. Etc. Between uses, the Cat was kept in a particular red baize cloth bag. So spilling a secret which got someone in trouble and resulted in their being flogged was called "Letting the Cat Out Of The Bag."

There is no "rope" aboard a ship, except in bulk storage. If it is cut to length for a purpose, it is invariably a "Line."

There are no closets on a ship. There are Storerooms. Any container where something is stored is called a "Locker." Personal Locker, Paint Locker, Life Jacket Locker, etc.

The Officer's common dining room and socialization space is called The Wardroom.

The Chief Petty Officers' equivalent is officially called The Chief's Mess, but is often called "The Goat Locker."

A bathroom is always a "Head". This dates back to when the sanitary facility was nothing more than a bench with a hole in it, built over the water well forward of the flare of the hull (at the Head of the ship), exposed to the weather. As sailing ships traveled downwind, placing the Head forward kept the smell downwind from the crew. Take a look at the movie *Master & Commander* with Russell Crowe. There is a scene with his ship sailing a snowstorm, and a shot of the ship's bow features a sailor on the head, with his breeches around his knees.

A shower compartment in the head is sometimes referred to as "The Rain Locker."

The ship's medical personnel are usually enlisted men in the Hospital Corpsman (HM) rating. (Very large ships may have a medical doctor and occasionally a dentist, but I never served on a ship with either. I was a destroyerman.) They are who you see when you report to morning sick call complaining of any ailment. And because sailors historically occasionally (okay, frequently) developed cases of venereal disease after going ashore, the Corpsman is also known as "The Pecker Checker."

Sailors in technical ratings, especially electronics, are known as "Twidgets". Engineers are known as "Snipes." Some ratings have their own epithets. Hull Technicians (who perform piping repairs, including sanitary systems, are sometimes called "Turd Chasers." Signalmen (who used hand-held flags to communicate in semaphore) were called "Skivvy Wavers" (an allusion to waving around underwear as makeshift signal flags.) Radiomen used to be called "Spark Shooters" and often were called the general nickname "Sparks". Ditto Boatswains Mates – "Boats" and Gunners Mates – "Guns". But Boatswain's Mates and their non-rated junior enlisted men supervisees are sometimes disparagingly called "Deck Apes" (usually not within their hearing.)

A sailor known as a man who partied very hard when ashore was called a "Liberty Hound" or a "Steamer."

"Liberty" is a period of off-duty recreation ashore measured in hours. No formal orders are cut and the man is instantly re-callable if needed or if he does something he shouldn't. "Shore Leave" is longer, and is more formal, with actual orders being issued, allowing travel and documenting that he is NOT expected to return before his orders say he is.

Dust bunnies, those little gray tumbleweeds of dust and hair which one finds behind furniture and in frame bays and overheads which haven't been cleaned recently enough, are known to sailors as "Ghost Turds".

A piece of firefighting equipment, the Fog Applicator, is a long pipe with a bend in it, and a bulbous bronze nozzle on the end. Sailors irreverently call this a "Donkey Dick." (I have no idea why.)

The classic Navy soft drink, a chilled beverage made from powder (analogous to Kool-Aid), usually kept in dispensers on the mess decks and available at all times, is known as "Bug Juice." Bug Juice comes in several garish colors, none of which is found in nature. And when spilled, it makes an awful, sticky mess. It has been used to polish brass, as it is mildly acidic.

Creamed Chipped Beef on Toast (one perennially favorite Navy breakfast item) is usually called "SOS" – for "S&^% On A Shingle"

Beef Roulades (a sort of oblong patty of roast beef in brown gravy) are known as "Nairobi Trail Markers." I'll leave it to you to figure out the visual reference.

Brussels Sprouts (almost always soggy, overcooked and bitter by the time they are served on the Mess Line, and pretty much universally despised by sailors are called "Little Green Balls Of Death."

Cheeseburgers are called "Sliders", as they are usually so greasy, they will slide right off the plate if the ship rolls.

Practical Jokes can be pretty funny too. Sending a junior man down to the Fireroom to fetch a "BT punch" would result in a large Boiler Technician (BT) giving him a bruising punch to the upper arm. Sending him to a Boatswains Mate for "fifty feet of shoreline" was good for a laugh (when no shoreline would be visible for a thousand sea miles.) And junior sailors would occasionally be told that the USN used a novel method of delivering personal mail to ships. A watertight buoy would be anchored in a particular spot in the ocean, and the ship's mail would be dropped off there by a support ship, where it could be retrieved as the ship passed by. More than a few junior sailors have been stationed topside with binoculars on "Mail Buoy Watch" to help find the elusive buoy.

Another practical joke was hilarious, unless you were the intended recipient. My first ship was a guided missile cruiser, and she was designed and commissioned in the early 1960s. She was 533 feet long, so was a pretty big ship. When she was built, interior communications were still fairly primitive, and having the ability to pass written messages and reports quickly about the ship was deemed useful. So the ship was fitted with an actual, no-kidding pneumatic tube system. Large Pipes ran between several critical control stations including the Bridge, CIC, Damage Control Central, the Radio Room, The Engineering Central Control Station, and a few other spaces. The pipes had very gentle bends along their lengths and a manifold system whereby they could be selectively connected. A clear plastic capsule about a foot long and about five inches in diameter could be loaded with a paper message, the top screwed on, and the capsule placed in the tube, with the breech door shut behind it. With the pull of a handle, compressed air shot the capsule, called a "bunny" through the piping to the other end, where it exited the tube and was caught in a basket, passing the message very rapidly. The whole shebang was called "The Bunny Tube" system by the sailors. You may have seen one still in use at a bank drive-up teller window.

Unfortunately the "Bunny Tube" could also be used for evil purposes. In this primitive time, the Radio Room handled all printed message traffic on large teletype machines called AN/UGC-6 Teletypes. These behemoths were about the size of a small upright piano, and they chattered away night and day printing off incoming message traffic received by radio signals. As they printed the message in readable form, they also created a digital record of it by punching holes in a stiff paper tape about an inch wide, with patterns of holes representing each character of the message on the long roll of tape. The paper tape could be torn off and retained, or run through another machine to reload the message for correction or retransmission. Punching the holes in the paper tape left millions of little discs of stiff paper about two millimeters in diameter, called "chads" and the Radio Room manufactured chad in huge quantities each day. It was collected in bags and eventually destroyed. One of the cruelest practical jokes was to quietly squirrel away a pound or two of chad, and to wait until a work space served by the Bunny Tube system was just finishing up a periodic waxing of the linoleum tile deck. If you put the chad in a paper bag, cut long slits in the sides, and then placed the resulting "chad bomb" on top of a bunny in the tube, it could be shot into the target space with considerable force and it would shower its contents onto the deck near the tube station, into the wet wax. Crewmen learned to secure the Bunny Tube when waxing fairly quickly...and I have never seen a sailor move more quickly than when he was just finishing up applying the wet wax and he heard the whoosh of an approaching bunny.

One very junior engineer on my first ship was sent to borrow a Stroboscopic Tachometer (called a StroboTach) from another work center. When he got there, the young man didn't really know what he had been sent to get, and did the best he could. After the laughter died away (which took some time), the equipment in question was ever more known aboard that ship as a "Scrotum Tech."

On my last ship, the crew was small and unusually close-knit. And one night, the 1989 movie *Bill & Ted's Excellent Adventure* was shown on the mess decks, cracking everybody up with the antics of then very young Keanu Reeves and Alex Winter. For many weeks after, crew members played air guitar or repeated any of a dozen gag lines from the movie. My personal favorite: "Strange things are afoot at the Circle K," used whenever anything unusual was happening.

Some other everyday expressions, translated from Sailorese:

"What the hell, over?" = "Why did you just do that?"

FIGMO = "Eff it, I got my orders." (which means, "I don't care, I'm leaving the ship soon anyway.")

DILLIGAF? = "Do I look like I give a F%$#?"

CHAPTER 53

Serving An Admiral

One of my most enjoyable tours on active duty was as Aide and Flag Lieutenant to a Rear Admiral. All Flag Officers in the USN rate a personal staff in addition to the command staff assigned to whatever unit they command. In my case, I was assigned to Commander, Service Group TWO, in Norfolk. VA. The Commander at that time was RADM M.E. "Jim" Toole, USN.

The Admiral: RADM Toole was a very interesting man. He obtained his commission though the NROTC. He was a Surface Warfare Officer, who had in his time commanded a River Division of PBRs (riverine gunboats) in Vietnam, a Destroyer Escort, a guided Missile Destroyer, and later a Guided Missile Cruiser. Upon selection to flag rank, he was given command of SERVGRU TWO, which was a collection of support vessels of the Atlantic Surface Forces. These ships included Destroyer Tenders, Oilers, Ammunition Ships, Refrigerated Stores ships , Salvage and Recovery ships, and a Mobile Diving and Salvage Unit, all organized into three squadrons. This was the logistics support arm of the Atlantic Fleet, as well as the NATO Strike Fleet, Atlantic. A wise man once said "Amateurs debate tactics. Professionals worry about logistics." This is exactly right, and it was a huge responsibility. RADM Toole was a very tough, very capable and extremely intelligent officer. He was a voracious reader and serious student of history, with tremendous powers of recall of details. His father had been an actual horse cavalryman who was sent into Mexico to chase down Pancho Villa! As befitting a Vietnam War "brown water navy" veteran (he is favorably mentioned in the book *Rogue Warrior*, by Dick Marcinko) he was all business and no bullshit. He demanded accountability from those who he led.

And he was known for convening disciplinary hearings (Admiral's Mast) for a large number of officers of the group whose ships had problems or incidents. He was not at all averse to calling senior officers in front of the "Long Green Table" and rendering punitive judgment when it was called for. He was also very tough in his role of logistician for the NATO Strike Fleet. He was the first USN admiral to make the annual wargamers at the Naval War College consider the LOGISTICS aspects of their battle simulations. These annual wargames were factored in to force levels and tactical plans; prior to RADM Toole, it was all about who shot who, with how many missiles or torpedoes. But Admiral Toole made them be realistic. *"OK, how many missiles did USS Belknap fire yesterday in battle? 62, sir. OK then how did she just fire 40 more? She only had 18 remaining!......Well, sir, she replenished last night! From whom? USS Nitro, sir! No, Nitro departed the battle group yesterday morning to refill her magazines in Iceland, she wasn't there. Uhhhhhh......OK, so Belknap was sunk, then."* BIG DIFFERENCE IN OUTCOME, based upon logistic realities instead of simply throwing around imaginary missiles. RADM Toole spoke his mind and did what he thought was right. I really liked and respected him, and enjoyed being his Flag Lieutenant. He had a flamboyant personal style, too. He was single, and had a striking, well-endowed blonde girlfriend who was very impressive when they attended social events together. He was quite a guy. He was very good to me and I did my best to take good care of him.

Personal Staff: A Rear Admiral had a personal staff of four who reported directly to him: A Flag Secretary, A Flag Lieutenant/Aide, a Flag Writer and a Driver. The Flag Secretary was a Lieutenant Commander (Limited Duty Officer) who was an admin specialist, and handled the Admiral's personal correspondence as well as overseeing the Group's official paperwork. The Flag Writer was a First Class Petty Officer Yeoman (later a CPO) who typed, prepared low-level notes, and created drafts of some correspondence, and directly supervised the Driver, who was an E-3 Seaman whose job it was to drive the admiral to wherever he needed to go, and to keep the assigned pool vehicle clean and ready. And I was the Flag Lieutenant/Aide (more on this later.)

(Uniform and historical note: officers assigned as personal staff to a USN Admiral wear a distinctive item of uniform apparel called an aiguillette, on their left shoulder. It is a looped cord of blue and gold threads, with the number of loops signifying the rank of the admiral, corresponding to the number of stars he wears. In this way, the officer can immediately be identified as someone who is serving the immediate needs of an Admiral, and given appropriate priority. The dress aiguillette is extremely ornate, whereas the daily wear item is simpler. According to the history I was taught, the aiguillette has its historical origins in the 1300s. A very senior Spanish officer, the Duke of Medina Sedona, had a small elite bodyguard force of personal troops, who he used for important missions when required. And each man carried a small coil of rope around one shoulder at all times, as an insignia of his membership in that unit. And if the man ever failed to accomplish an assigned task, he was expected to immediately hang himself with that rope! Today's aiguillette is a stylized symbol of that ancient tradition.)

The Flag Lieutenant: How do you get this job? In my day, one civilian employee at the USN Bureau of Personnel was responsible for identifying officers whose records indicated good potential to be flag Aides. When an Admiral needed an Aide, she would send over several service record nominations for the Admiral to choose from, and he would pick one. I'm not sure how I got into that pile, but I'm glad I did. (I think Admiral Toole picked me because I got my commission from NROTC, and had been serving on a cruiser like the one he had commanded.) The job of the Flag Lieutenant (also known in Navy parlance as a "dog robber") is to take care of the Admiral's daily needs. To help him carry out his daily routine, and fetch him whatever he needs to do it. To get him to events on time, in proper uniform and knowing what he needs to know to be effective. To give him briefing materials and to track them when they are classified so they don't get compromised. To carry his bags, fetch his drinks, get him to the proper seat at the table, and do whatever is needed so that he looks omniscient, vice unprepared. To get his car serviced, to help him prepare for and carry out social events in his home when of an official nature. Basically, to help him make the most efficient use of his limited time, but doing WHATEVER he needs done to accomplish the mission. In return for this difficult, time-consuming job, the young officer is given a graduate-level education in big issues, learns how the Navy actually runs, sees and hears much of instructive value, and meets a lot of powerful people. The Admiral usually helps the officer get a career-enhancing next assignment (assuming that he has done well. Not everyone does.)

Pitfalls: I know of two Flag Lieutenants who didn't do well, and were fired from the job. One guy had a fender bender with the Admiral's official car while he was off using it without permission during a duty day. He knew that the Admiral had to have a car, and driving around in a badly dented vehicle wouldn't go unnoticed. So he rushed over to the base motor pool and demanded that they give him a new vehicle for the Admiral while they fixed the old one. He mentioned this to no one. And later that afternoon, the Admiral took the keys, drove himself to the golf course and opened the trunk, looking for his expensive set of golf clubs... which weren't there. They were still in the car over at the motor pool garage. Oops. You're fired.

The other one was my predecessor, who was already gone when I reported aboard to replace him. (That's never a good sign.) While some Admirals are notorious for firing their Aides at the first drop of a hat, Admiral Toole was more patient, but in the end the guy had to go. For starters, he apparently had legendary halitosis; this isn't a good reflection on the boss. Then the "Uniform Incident" happened. The Surface Forces Atlantic Ball is a major social event of the year. All the brass are there in resplendent seasonally-appropriate full dress uniform. Dinner, drinks, dancing, major schmoozing, it's a big deal. So the Aide has helped the Admiral prepare. And upon the hour, the Admiral pulls up in his car with his Girlfriend...and sees that he is in the WRONG uniform. He drops the Girlfriend off at the mall with his credit card to buy an appropriate evening dress (she is now angry, so buys a REALLY NICE ONE...on his dime.) He races back from Virginia Beach to Norfolk, changes into the right uniform, and speeds back to pick up the Girlfriend, who is now wearing *haute couture* and rocking the cleavage and mile-long legs on stiletto heels. And they are very late; so late that in fact they walk in and proceed to their head-table seats, right in the middle of Commander, Naval Surface Forces Atlantic (the Admiral's boss)'s speech...thereby causing quite a stir! No one remembers the slightest detail of the speech, ever. But they sure remember the entrance and the Girlfriend. But the straw that broke the Aide's back, so to speak, was the "NATO Speech Incident." It is a major briefing to a huge NATO annual fleet exercise staff. The Admiral is at the podium, addressing the assembled crowd of senior NATO officers, with dozens of admirals, generals and other seniors of several NATO countries listening to his presentation. My predecessor is sitting in his chair in the front row, aiguillette on his shoulder, with the Admiral's briefcase at his feet, in case he needs to provide any other materials. The room is crowded with a couple of hundred people and is quite warm. The Aide dozes off...and falls out of his front-row seat, onto the floor, as his (my) Admiral is speaking.

I reported in as the new Flag Lieutenant about a month later.

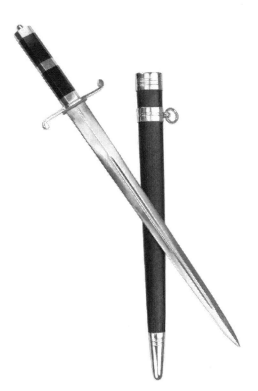

CHAPTER 54

Naval Edged Weapons

No single attribute has played a greater part in the survival of the human species and its ascendance to the top of the food chain than our ability to use tools. And the fundamental tool of the human animal is the edged weapon, or basically, the knife. The knife, and the opposable thumb with which to wield it, has been the single most important factor in human evolutionary achievement, the rise and fall of civilizations, the mastery of the environment and the elements. When things go south, there is no more important tool, even in the modern age, than the knife. All of which is a long way of saying that I like sharp, shiny things. Always have.

Weapons are very much designed with the understanding that their uses have the preservation of life itself at stake. Form follows function. Chipped stone first yielded to copper, then bronze, which yielded in time to iron, and then to increasingly better steels as technology and materials science progressed And most individual weapons are variations on a theme. The basic weapon? The knife. A sword? A long knife, the better to kill an enemy with from a bit further away. An axe? A knife on a stick. A spear? A knife on a loooong stick. An arrow? A small knife on a thin flying stick. A bullet? A knife you can throw really far and fast. Shrapnel? Lots of knives propelled by explosions. The knife is the mother of many weapons. And different cultures developed different designs, across many ages and based upon their way of fighting, in the context of their dress, tactics and environment.

In the modern age military, hand-held edged weapons are largely confined to uniformed ceremonial use (there are some exceptions among elite troops.) The US Army doesn't even train recruits in the use of the bayonet anymore. That's a pity. But there are certain weapons associated with each service's dress uniforms. The US Army has both an Officer's sword and an NCO sword. Both are saber designs, with curved blades and (ostensibly sharpened) false edges to be used to deliver fencing back cuts. The historical designs of both harken back to actual weapons that were used by actual soldiers, infantry and cavalry, in mortal combat. The USMC has an Officer's sword, and an NCO saber. Both are modeled after actual weapons, and the officer's sword is in fact a copy of a foreign weapon that was presented by a foreign potentate to a USMC officer, who then carried it as a trophy. The US Air Force has an Officer's sword. As the Air Force was born long after hand-to-hand combat by officers was passe', and they wanted to look different from the other services in their dress uniforms, so they chose a straight bladed semi-civilized design with a very small guard. It is basically a piece of costume jewelry. (To be fair, the

A Naval Cutlass

USAF also uses the Army officer's saber, as they grew out of the Army Air Corps.)

But the USN (and the British Royal Navy before it) has historically had three edged weapons associated with it, and many battles have seen their use. The three are the Dirk, the Cutlass and the Naval Officer's Sword. The design of each reflects the conditions of use which were expected. Combat on the deck of a warship is a very close, confined affair. Sailors would climb aboard their enemies' ship. There would be men cheek to jowl, with rigging, spars, equipment, sails and cannons all around them. There was simply little room to deliver wide, swinging, haymaker slashes. Attempting to do that could easily lead to your weapon catching on someone or something before it reached its intended target, and leaving you open to a killing blow. **So naval weapons mostly emphasized the thrust vice the slash.** This stroke could be delivered straight in, with a minimum of space and a quick economy of motion. It is also usually more deadly than a slash; slashes lead to painful bleeding which in time may lead to death, but more often lead to capitulation. Thrusts lead to hemorrhage, which quite usually leads to death, thereby conclusively winning the argument. (Historical digression: I once read a fascinating treatise by a noted martial artist, who posited that historically, cultures whose weapons and tactics favored the thrust conquered more, won more and lasted longer than cultures which emphasized the slash. The Chinese Jian, the Greek Xiphos, the Roman Gladius, the English Backsword and the moderately-curved Saber all saw empires rise behind their keen points. The Author "made his point", at least to me.)

The Dirk: The Dirk was normally carried by Midshipmen. As Midshipmen were typically young men in their early-late teens, they were not yet able to wield longer, heavier weapons, but still had to be able to defend themselves. A dirk is a smallish, straight bladed dagger with a needle point, and usually with a single sharpened edge and a double guard. It didn't slash well, but it pierced like nobody's business in a thrust.

The Cutlass: The Cutlass was usually wielded by common sailors, who had little formal instruction in fencing. Put a sword in the hands of an untrained man, and his usual instinct is to slash with it. So a short, heavy-bladed weapon with a massive handguard and a thrusting point was developed – the Cutlass. It could slash and thrust, had enough mass to cleave flesh and bone if a swing could be delivered, and it was short enough to allow use in close confines. (Some sailors were also issued pikes,

A Naval Officer's Sword

which are pure thrusting weapons akin to spears, and boarding axes. These axes were not for fighting *per se*; they were be used to cut down the enemies' supportive rigging, thereby dismasting their ship and winning the battle. But they were dandy for killing if you could get one into an enemy's skull.) So the cutlass became a traditional naval weapon, optimized for use in close quarters by a relatively unskilled man.

The Naval Officer's Sword: A Naval Officer was (and is) a gentleman. His education, therefore, included the manly art of fencing: fighting with a sword, like a gentleman. Thrust and parry, with only occasional subtle slashes as tactical elements. So a Naval Officer's sword followed a historical pattern called a spadroon – a longish, straight blade, with a keen point and a sharpened false (back) edge near the point, to allow back cuts. It had a stylized knucklebow and guard to protect the hand during parrying maneuvers, and featured nautical motifs as artistic embellishments. It was a poor slashing tool, but a very keen thrusting weapon, capable of running an opponent through with ease. Straight in, straight out, gurgle, thunk, fight over. Hoist the colors, splice the main brace, and start calculating a course back to home port.

VADM John D. Bulkeley, USN

CHAPTER 55

Meeting A Legend

In 1986, I was privileged to meet and have a conversation with a *bona fide* US Navy legend and hero of World War II. VADM John D. Bulkeley was a member of the U.S. Naval Academy graduating class of 1933. When World War II began for America on the 07th of December 1941, then-Lieutenant Bulkeley was in command of Motor Torpedo Boat Squadron Three, a group of six plywood PT boats, in Cavite, Philippines. These small, gallant little craft carried four torpedoes and several machine guns each, and were powered by gasoline engines. They were basically floating bombs, but could and did punch above their weight. The 1945 movie *They Were Expendable*, starring John Wayne and Robert Montgomery is a dramatization of these boats' service, and is a WWII classic film.

The US Navy in the Pacific had been decimated by the Pearl Harbor attacks, so even though the Navy brass had prior to this time not been particularly impressed by the PT boat concept, the little boats were pressed into service to attack Japanese shipping. They usually did so at night, and the tiny vessels and crews sank numerous Japanese warships and supply ships in the early years of the war. They took heavy casualties. But the PTs played a major role in disrupting Japanese supply efforts in battles in the Solomon Islands campaign, raiding Japanese convoys dubbed "The Tokyo Express" coming down "The Slot" as New Georgia Sound was known. Imagine being told to get aboard your little plywood boat and sally forth to attack a task force of Japanese destroyers and cruisers, by necessity "up close and personal." This was a contact sport, not for the faint of heart. And LT Bulkeley was right in the middle of it, leading these missions into curtains of heavy fire and taking the fight to the Japanese to good effect.

In March of 1942, LT Bulkeley got a most unusual mission order. And on the 12th of March, he took PT-41 and three other boats of his squadron to Corregidor Island, at the mouth of Manila Bay, and embarked General of the Armies Douglas MacArthur, his wife and child, and members of his household and staff. The Philippines were about to fall to the Japanese Army, and President Roosevelt had ordered MacArthur to evacuate from the Philippines to prevent his capture or death. LT Bulkeley and his PTs transported these key personnel to Mindanao, from where they were flown to safety in Australia. And in recognition of his gallant combat service before and during that operation, LT Bulkeley was awarded the Medal Of Honor by President Roosevelt, becoming one of the highest decorated officers in US Navy history. His career decorations include that Medal of Honor, the Navy Cross, two Distinguished Service Crosses, the Silver Star, the Legion of Merit and the Purple Heart. Bulkeley is the man who, after meeting US Ambassador Joseph Kennedy in September 1942, recruited future President John F. Kennedy into the USN PT Boat service. He survived the war and went on to lead a stellar naval career, rising to the rank of Vice Admiral, and initially retiring in 1975. But in the early 1980s, he was recalled to active duty to lead the USN's Board of Inspection and Survey (INSURV.) This organization thoroughly inspects every Navy ship about every five years, to document its material readiness in minute detail, and to advise hard decisions about the ship's fitness for further duty. It is a job for a man who has tremendous focus, a pugnacious tenacity and a No-BS approach to the facts. VADM Bulkeley was just such a man. He was known as a fighter, and a no-nonsense commander.

It was in this capacity that our conversation took place. I was Flag Lieutenant and Aide to a Rear Admiral in command of a large Group of logistics supply ships. One of them was undergoing her INSURV inspection, and some significant problems had come to light. VADM Bulkeley was not pleased, and hard decisions were going to have to be made about costs, accountability and the further service of the vessel. The Admiral and I reported aboard the Destroyer Tender that VADM Bulkeley was using as his temporary office during that inspection, and we were shown into his cabin. There he was, the Legend himself, in an old, faded khaki uniform made soft by countless washings. His hair was gray, his face weathered by nearly 55 years of naval service, including several years of pitched combat. He greeted the Admiral with the respect due to his rank and command position. He then fixed me with a steely gaze, his eyes penetrating and belying a less-than-gentle spirit. I was in awe. And then he spoke: "You can go now." And I replied: "Aye, aye, sir." I did a smart about face and departed the cabin, leaving the two Admirals to their discussions.

I didn't say it was a LONG conversation.

CHAPTER 56

Jump-Starting
a Hydrofoil

USS TAURUS (PHM-3)

In 1990, I got to experience a most unusual triumph of creative thinking as applied to Naval Engineering. It was even more remarkable as a shining example of sea service cooperation.

The little city of Port Lavaca, Texas is about 130 miles southwest of Houston, up a long, straight shipping channel cutting through the dusty, arid south Texas landscape. The port services several major industrial entities, including Alcoa Aluminum, Formosa Plastics, and DuPont. In 1990, it was a sleepy little burg of about 11,000 people. But it was celebrating the Sesquicentennial of its founding in 1840. And the City Fathers had asked the US Navy to help them observe the occasion by sending a warship to take part.

I was serving as Executive Officer and Navigator of a 132-foot Guided Missile Hydrofoil, USS TAURUS (PHM-3). One of our sister ships happened to be captained by a native son of Port Lavaca. He had accepted (in fact, had probably finagled) the assignment to take his ship there for a multi-day port visit during the Sesquicentennial Celebration. The ship would give public tours (thereby putting a positive face on the USN and perhaps inspiring a few future enlistments,) and pump a few federal dollars and sailor's paychecks into the local economy. Everybody would have a great time.

Unfortunately for them, our sister ship experienced some kind of mechanical problem which could not be immediately repaired. So our parent Squadron reached out to us with literally a day or two's notice, asking if we would pick up her commitment to visit Port Lavaca, so that the USN would not have to suffer an embarrassing cancellation. The mighty TAURUS did as she always did, and met the challenge with grace and ability. Off we flew from Key West to South Texas, 958 nautical miles across the crystal blue of the Gulf of Mexico. The town was very pleased to host us, and we were eagerly toured by several thousand visitors over the next few days. I had actually conned the Captain into letting me transport my motorcycle, a Honda Hurricane 600CC sport bike, on the main deck, and I roared off to San Antonio to visit the parents of my best friend in high school. We had a nice visit, and I miraculously didn't kill myself riding across Texas at very high speeds.

The PEGASUS-class hydrofoils were a unique hybrid of aircraft and ship. One of the peculiar aspects of the design was that we had three separate electrical systems. The largest, main ship's power, was 400hz AC. Your normal house current is 60hz AC. 400Hz is much more suitable for powering delicate electronics, which the ship was packed with, as it features a much smoother sine wave and fewer fluctuations. Lots of the ship's equipment was therefore specially built to run on 400hz. (The galley toaster sounded like a jet engine warming up when you inserted slices of bread!) We made our own electricity using two Ships Service Power Units (SSPUs, pronounced "spoos") which were small gas turbine-driven generators analogous to APUs on an aircraft. We split and transformed a small portion of our power off into a 60hz convenience circuit, so certain appliances like electric razors, power tools, etc could be powered and charged. And we had a 28-volt DC system which was served by some onboard battery banks and recharged by our ships' generators. This circuit powered critical instrumentation, emergency lighting and generator start functions.

Normally, the ship ran the SSPUs only when underway, as they consumed jet fuel and created a good deal of topside exhaust noise. When inport, we would plug into a Shore Power Cart, which was a specialized portable transformer system. These were unique to the hydrofoils, as they were designed to take normal shore power and convert it into the 400hz electricity we used. But there was a problem. Somehow, the Shore Power Cart we needed had not made it from Key West to Port Lavaca in time to support us for the visit. We ran one of the two SSPUs full time, and no doubt the attendant noise pollution put a bit of a damper on the celebrations close to the ship. But on the last day, things went pear-shaped.

The SSPU also provided compressed air which we used for starting our main engine, a General Electric LM-2500 gas turbine. You absolutely could not start the turbine without an SSPU running. Somehow, the running SSPU shut down, and we were suddenly cold and dark. OK, no problem. We could start the other SSPU using the 28v DC battery bank......except that somehow, a switch had been misaligned for the duration of our port visit and the batteries had not been charging for three days, as we had thought. And they retained insufficient charge to start a SSPU. We were well and truly out of electricity.

Now this was a major embarrassment. It looked like the Mighty TAURUS was going to have to sit there, cold and dark, waiting for a couple of days until a shore power cart could be towed all the way from Key West to Port Lavaca – a one-way trip of 1474 miles, or about half-way across these United States. Ain't nobody happy about this.

Enter the hero – USS TAURUS's Chief Engineer (CHENG.) This excellent officer was actually a Lieutenant (Junior Grade) of the U.S. Coast Guard, assigned to us on exchange duty. He didn't know much about (and was there to learn about) the US Navy, but he was an excellent marine engineer who had considerable seagoing experience for his years. He was a heck of a nice guy, well-respected, and a creative thinker. We sat around a table in the Port Office, with the Captain, the Chief Engineer, The Port Captain, and the City Fathers, trying to figure out how we were going to get the situation resolved. The Texans were willing to do anything they could to support us. "What do you need?" they asked. "Well, technically, we need 28 volts of Direct Current, supplied at high amperage" said the CHENG. Where could we get high-amperage DC? Then a curious expression came over his face. "Do you happen to have a large portable industrial welding rig?"

he asked. "This is an industrial port, you're dang tootin' we do!" came the reply. About a half-hour later, a big dually work truck pulled alongside, towing a sizeable portable welding rig. An old, weather-beaten cowboy hopped out, in his faded jeans, work shirt, battered stetson and dusty cowboy boots. He fired off the generator which powered the welder, and we connected cables to the ship, after setting the rig to produce 28 volts of output. Crossing our fingers, we turned up the amperage and threw the breaker. **WhooooooooooOOOOOOOOOO** went the SSPU, and with a belch of exhaust smoke, it roared into normal operation. Then: **WHOOOOOOOOMMMMMMMMMMM** went the main turbine, adding its cacophonous roar to the scene. And within an hour, we were flying down the ship channel and into the Gulf of Mexico, homeward bound. Three cheers for the US Coast Guard!

CHAPTER 57

Refugees

One of the more poignant aspects of operating in the Florida Straits during the 1970s – 1990s was the occasional encounter with Cuban refugees at sea. Many thousands of Cubans, desperate for freedom and sick of living under the nightmare shadow of communism, took to the open ocean in a wide variety of watercraft. In decrepit fishing craft, other small boats and even home-built rafts, they braved the treacherous straits and tried to reach America and freedom. One brave young man picked his weather conditions correctly and traversed the entire 90-mile strait on a windsurfer. Some lucky ones made it; no one knows how many thousands died trying. It was a humanitarian crisis and an awful tragedy. And US law at the time said that if they made it to shore and touched land, they were allowed to stay, but if they were apprehended at sea, they would be returned to Cuba. Upon their return, they could expect prosecution and confinement in a labor reeducation camp. Like despotic tyrants everywhere, Castro and his communist minions were harsh and unforgiving.

One day in 1989, *USS TAURUS* (PHM-3) was operating south of Key West on counter-narcotics patrol, with a US Coast Guard Law Enforcement Detachment aboard. As we passed by some deep-sea charter fishing boats with paying customers aboard, we received a call on our bridge-to-bridge radio. The caller informed us that a Cuban fishing boat further out in the straits had recovered some refugees from the water and needed assistance. They gave us the radio channel information where the fishing boat could be contacted. We started trying to contact the vessel.

A big problem quickly became apparent. The Cuban vessel (which was using a fake name on the radio) spoke no English. Zero. Zip. Zilch. And no one aboard my ship was fluent in Spanish. Well, among my limited toolkit inventory, I had a minor in Spanish language from university. I never was what you might call fluent, and had not used my limited skills in several years, but there was nothing else to do, so I gamely grabbed the microphone and tried to make contact. (For what it is worth, Cuban Spanish is quite different from either pure Castilian from Spain, and from the more mellifluous Spanish spoken across Latin America. It sounds mushy and indistinct by comparison.) In time, I was able to make a very rudimentary contact with the boat in question. They did indeed have six refugees aboard who needed assistance, and they were able to laboriously pass us the numbers giving their geographic position in Latitude and Longitude. Off we flew to the rescue.

We were able to make rendezvous, and found five men and a woman who had made it about two-thirds of the way across the Florida Straits in a 14-foot open wooden boat propelled by a small outboard motor before running out of gas. The boat was painted a dull gray, making it harder to see on the ocean. They were dressed lightly, in t-shirts and trousers, and had a few plastic jugs of water and one gray blanket which they were using both for warmth and to hide under if Cuban search aircraft passed overhead. They were happy to come aboard our ship, and the Cuban fishing boat was glad to be rid of them, so that they did not run afoul of Cuban laws. We fed them as we returned to Key West, and turned them over to the Border Patrol pierside upon arrival. They no doubt hoped that they had reached Paradise. But we sadly knew that according to US law, they ultimately would be deported back to Cuba. I hope that in time they attained something like freedom.

CHAPTER 58

Forgotten History

I have always loved history, and naval history in particular. No event has ever had a greater impact on the U.S. Navy than the Japanese attack on Pearl Harbor on Sunday, December 07th, 1941. The reminders of that attack are still very much visible. I have visited Pearl Harbor many times, I underwent Refresher Training there in 1988, and I have reenlisted a couple of sailors aboard the USS ARIZONA Memorial. Navy ships still render passing honors to that sunken battleship entombing over 900 sailors as they steam past it.

A little-remembered aspect of the Japanese attack is that they deployed five two-man mini-submarines as part of the attack force. These vessels were new technology at the time, and had a very distinctive size and shape, with two vertically-mounted torpedo tubes protruding from their bows. One of the subs was sunk outside the harbor entrance that morning by the destroyer USS WARD, which in so doing fired the opening shots of America's participation in World War II. Two of the subs actually penetrated the Harbor defenses and recent historical research indicates that they probably hit the battleships USS WEST VIRGINIA and USS OKLAHOMA with torpedoes. And one boat washed ashore on the coast of Oahu, having failed to clear the reef and make it into the harbor. That boat, the HA-19, was recovered, and while one crewman had died, the other, Ensign Kazuo Sakamaki, was apprehended and became America's first captured Japanese POW. A photo of HA-19 stranded on the beach is one of the iconic images of America's first day of the war.

Flash forward forty-eight years. As Executive Officer of *USS TAURUS* (PHM-3), I was based and quartered at Naval Station Key West's Trumbo Point facility in 1989. Trumbo Point is an old seaplane base. This is where officer housing, the BOQ and the piers which were home to the USN's Hydrofoil Squadron were located. It is also home to the US Army Special Forces Dive School. I enjoyed commuting on foot, walking back and forth between my ship and my quarters, past the dive school and its then-antiquated dive tower, which was a tall water-filled tank with an old diesel submarine escape trunk mounted at its base, and where SF divers learned how to perform scuba lockouts/reentries into submerged submarines.

One day, out of boredom, I took a different route home, exploring behind some close-to-abandoned buildings on the base. And I stopped dead in my tracks, looking through a rusty chain-link fence at a piece of forgotten naval history. For there sat the

HA-19 today

HA-19, with its unmistakable profile and bow torpedo tubes. A unique and priceless artifact, she was just lying there, canted at a slight list, rusting silently away. Apparently she had spent some years on static display at the nearby Key West Submarine Base, and when that base was closed she had been hauled into the vacant lot and left to rot. It was like seeing a ghost of Naval History, footsteps from my own front door.

Happily, HA-19 was not lost to posterity. She was eventually relocated to the National Museum of the Pacific War in Fredericksburg, Texas in 1991. Her surviving crewman visited her there that same year. She has been nicely restored on her exterior, and can be seen there today, looking much as she did on the morning of December 07th, 1941.

USS TAURUS (PHM-3) in her prime. Note the proud "Fruit Salad"

CHAPTER 59

Fruit Salad.
The Battle "E"

Military uniforms and insignia are designed to convey a good deal of information about the wearer in visual form, rapidly and distinctively. Dress uniforms, with all of the wearer's badges of rank, emblems of qualification and ribbons or medals of awards displayed on them, enable the knowledgeable observer to tell instantly what the wearer has done, and where he has served. The colorful array of ribbons and devices is sometimes referred to as "fruit salad."

Ships also display a record of their achievements, proudly posted where they can be seen. These include unit awards, like the Meritorious Unit Commendation, the Navy Unit Commendation, and various campaign operations, which are usually displayed by painting facsimiles of their ribbons on the superstructure. Also proudly displayed are cyclic Departmental Awards, which represent tested and demonstrated excellence in such key skills as Damage Control, Engineering, Electronic Warfare, Navigation, Gunnery, etc. These are usually painted emblems or the Letter "E" painted in colors specific to their departments (green for Operations, Red for Engineering, etc.) The Big Daddy of them all is the Battle Effectiveness award (in my day called the Battle Efficiency award, or "Battle E.") Presented to only one ship per squadron, the Battle E marks the ship which as been adjudged to have performed the best over a specific year. It is a keen competition among sister ships to earn and display the distinction. It is marked by a large white "E" on the superstructure, and a small red triangular pennant with a black circle on it, called "the Meatball" which is flown from the mainmast truck. I was honored to have served aboard two Battle "E" winners, and proudly wore that ribbon on my uniform until retirement.

I distinctly remember the evaluation cycle which ended in December 1989. My ship, USS TAURUS (PHM-3) had been doing very well, and was a strong contender for the Battle "E" award. Several of our sister ships had had various misfortunes, and were not really believed to be in the running. USS PEGASUS (PHM-1) was lackluster at best. Two other sisters had run aground, at the same spot in the channel into Morehead City, NC. The one ship that we thought might be in serious contention with us was USS AQUILA (PHM-4). A fine ship, AQUILA had worked hard, done well and she looked great. My XO counterpart aboard her was and is a close friend.

The appointed day came for the announcement of the Battle E award...and in an inexplicable effort to improve morale among the *USS PEGASUS's* crew (which had been somewhat demoralized, as she was so often mechanically broken that she had gone almost nowhere and done almost nothing the entire year) **the Squadron chose her for the honor.** About five minutes after the announcement, I was sitting in irate disbelief when I got a call from the quarterdeck telling me "Sir, the XO of the *AQUILA* is on his way down to see you." My friend Brad burst into my stateroom/office, eyes ablaze. Shutting the door, he turned to face me and exclaimed "WE WAS ROBBED!" I couldn't agree more, then and now.

But justice was eventually done. Not long after she was given the Battle "E", *PEGASUS* underwent a major inspection, and she did extremely poorly, in several aspects. It was a major

USS ARIES (PHM-5) today. She has seen better days.

embarrassment for the ship and the Squadron. And the *PEGASUS's* Commanding Officer, rightly displeased, lowered the boom on his low-performing crew. HE MADE THEM PAINT OVER THE BATTLE "E" AND HAUL DOWN THE MEATBALL. He wouldn't let them display the award as he felt they were undeserving of it, and he only let them re-affix those marks to the ship when he felt their performance had significantly improved. And *USS TAURUS*, continuing her excellent performance, deservedly earned the Battle "E" the following cycle.

Navy units also display individual achievement when earned, in conformance with a very old tradition of keeping score and counting coup. Pilots paint an emblem for each kill on their fuselage. Destroyers paint little emblems for subs or ships sunk, targets attacked, etc. And the Hydrofoils, so often employed in counter-narcotics operations, affixed unique emblems representing the drug busts they made. These were little marijuana leaves, or snowflakes to represent cocaine seizures. The first photo is USS TAURUS in her prime, proudly displaying her "fruit salad." The second photo is the only remaining PHM, USS ARIES (PHM-5) which was saved from scrapping, privately purchased, and is now being kept as a museum up a river in Missouri. She is not looking her best these days.

CHAPTER 60

The Perils of a Darkened Bridge

Navy ships operating at night maintain a strict condition of darkened ship. Ideally, other than the tri-colored standard navigation lights, no other light should show topside. (Aircraft carriers and logistic ships have numerous task lights which make them look like massive oil rigs, but all other ships are very careful about this.) The ship's bridge is likewise kept very dark at night, with only a few dim indicator lights and displays, so that the watchstanders can see out into the dark ocean as keenly as possible. An officer coming up on bridge watch at night makes sure that his eyes are already adapted to night vision before he relieves the watch, so that he is prepared to see objects in the water and unlighted vessels with which he may collide. He also performs a period of acclimation to the current conditions, and observes and mentally notes all aspects of his orders, the ship's operating condition, and the environment. Typically, he arrives on the bridge about a half hour early, so he can be fully up to speed and ready before he relieves the watch on time.

One of my shipmates on my first ship was our Chief Engineer (CHENG.) An excellent officer, he had been assigned to an aged Guided Missile Destroyer, and when she was decommissioned, he received orders to our ship as Main Propulsion Assistant. He was so good that the Captain fleeted him up to Chief Engineer when the outgoing CHENG departed. About the only flaw in this officer's stellar abilities was that he enjoyed dipping smokeless tobacco. He always had a can of Skoal or Copenhagen in his back pocket, and usually had a big wad in his cheek, busily spitting a brown stream from time to time as he did his thing of keeping the lights on and the screws going roundy-roundy.

One extremely dark night, he was about to be relieved at midnight as Officer of the Deck (OOD) on the inky black darkened bridge. He had spent the entire 20-24 watch with a big cheek-full of Cope. The ocean was calm and the ship's motion was easy, so he had been spitting into an empty soda can, which at this point was pretty full after a four-hour watch. He had it sitting on the bridge railing on centerline, where he stood by the pilothouse pelorus.

The oncoming Officer of the Deck was likewise an excellent shipmate. A tall, lanky African American, he had played basketball at the Naval Academy. Soft-spoken but competent, he was hard to rattle and unlikely to show much emotion or get riled about anything. He had risen early, dressed, and arrived early to the bridge to perform his period of watch turnover. To help him stay awake on the midwatch, he had opened a cold can of Dr. Pepper and brought it up to the bridge with him. He stood next to the CHENG in the darkness, receiving his turnover briefing, and he set his Dr. Pepper on the bridge railing in the stygian darkness.

Yes, you guessed it. He grabbed the wrong can and took a big swig. After the immediate projectile vomiting ceased, his stream of outraged, incensed profanity spewed forth with equal impetus. His Naval Academy education had certainly equipped him with a sound grasp of that specialized vocabulary, and even enlisted sailors with decades at sea were impressed. The CHENG was contrite and apologetic, the can of spit was thrown overboard, the bridge deck was cleaned and life went on.

Strangely, the Midwatch OOD wasn't at breakfast in the wardroom the next morning. I guess he had no appetite.

USCG Aerostat Vessel

CHAPTER 61

Flying Food Service

The PEGASUS-class Guided Missile Hydrofoils were small ships, with small crews. Five officers and nineteen enlisted men were assigned to each and operated them at high speeds and in moderately severe sea states. They were a blast to serve aboard. One inescapable fact of Navy service is that the sailors have to eat! Their contract of enlistment guarantees them a place to sleep and three proper meals a day. Realizing that sea service is arduous and uncomfortable, the Navy does its best to provide enjoyable, tasty and nourishing meals (with varying degrees of success.) The Hydrofoils were so small that bunk and locker space per man was actually less than onboard a modern submarine. The Captain had a tiny private stateroom. The other four officers shared a single bunkroom, the Chief Petty Officers had an even smaller space and the individual sailor had a bunk bed smaller than a coffin. Quarters were very tight.

The galley where all the food for this crew was prepared was a masterpiece of efficient space utilization. It was a stainless-steel and aluminum cubicle about the size of a single sleeper compartment on a train, yet it had to serve 24 men three meals a day. There was only one cook assigned to each ship. A rated Mess Management Specialist (MS) this was invariably an E-6 First Class Petty Officer or E-7 Chief Petty Officer. As we were not manned with a Hospital Corpsman, the cook was also cross-trained as an Emergency Medical technician. In the event of combat casualties, he would have been treating the wounded on the mess deck tabletops. And he was solely responsible for feeding the crew every day at sea. Some times this was harder than others.

I remember one day in particular. We were on extended Anti-Drug patrol in the Caribbean Sea, and the weather was exceptionally foul. We were having to loiter in our patrol area for several days, so had to operate hullborne at slow speeds in the high seas and rainy winds, using only our diesel waterjets for propulsion. This meant our small ship was being rocked, rolled, twisted, spindled and pitched like any conventional ship, but we were lighter and smaller than most. The old *Mal-De-Mer*, or seasickness, was definitely having its way with any members of the crew who were prone to it. Lots of barfing was going on. I certainly was doing my share of it as usual.

Throughout my career, I was certainly as prone to seasickness as anybody aboard, maybe more than most. I have contributed much to the sea levels of several oceans. It is an awful feeling, made worse by the knowledge that once it kicks in, the conditions which caused it are not likely to abate any time soon. You are going to suffer...for days. And you still have to perform your duties and stand your watches, if necessary with a bucket tied around your neck. You sometimes are afraid that you AREN'T going to die from it, and it goes on and on and on...cold sweats, headaches, dry heaves and all.

On this day, I was sitting at the mess decks table with the cook, who was a recently-promoted Chief Petty Officer (MSC). I was reviewing the Plan of the Day and needed to know what the planned meal menus were, so we could inform the crew of what they had to look forward to throwing up later. I was also responsible for ensuring that they were adequately fed. As the ship corkscrewed wildly and we both turned several shades of bilious green, I asked the Chief what he planned to cook for dinner (as if anyone would want to eat it, but that is beside the point – they have to have the option if they so desire.)

The Chief, who was nearing retirement age, was a good-ol'-boy from Louisiana, with the Red Beans and Rice prowess and Southern drawl to prove it. He lifted his head from where he had been resting it on the table, looked at me with bleary eyes, and said *"well, Ah was gonna open up a bag of chips."* He meant it. He was going to simply put out an open bag of potato chips and have the drink dispenser full for self-service. As my stomach did aerobatic flip-flops, I hated to tell him that that wasn't going to cut it, and that he had to prepare a hot meal (that almost no one would want to eat, but it was what it was.) I did my duty and he did his. Life went on and in time, we went foilborne and resumed something akin to normal human existence.

Later that same patrol, we were nearing the end of our stored provisions, and a bit low on fuel. The PHMs were small enough that we only had room for about ten days' worth of food stores. But the Navy wanted us to stay put. Things were about to get uncomfortable AND hungry. In company near us was a US Coast Guard Aerostat Support Vessel. Originally built as an Offshore Supply Vessel to logistically support oil rigs, it had a broad afterdeck and a raised swiveling platform and pylon which was now home to a big helium blimp with a search radar suspended beneath it. The blimp would be allowed to go hundreds of feet aloft tethered by a steel cable, and the radar would allow detection of low-flying aircraft and surface vessels far beyond visual range. The ASV also still had most of her storeroom spaces, fuel tanks and other equipment which had been needed to keep an offshore oil rig working 24/7. A few calls were made, and the ASV indicated that she would be happy to pass us some fuel and food supplies if we would come get them. This had never been done before, but we did it. We steamed close alongside, and matched her speed. She passed us a hose, we hooked it up and she pumped us a load of fuel. Then she sent over some hand-tended lines, and tied on some plastic garbage bags full of loaves of bread, jars of peanut butter, saltine crackers, milk, beverage powder and other staples of life at sea. We became the first PHM to replenish underway from an ASV. Several of our sister ships subsequently exercised this capability as well. And it gave the PHM Squadron an additional mission edge.

CHAPTER 62

The Ball Cap

The Executive Officer (XO) on a ship is generally supposed to be the Bad Guy. The Second-In-Command, he roams the ship, keeping all in order, finding all the little discrepancies and faults, and issuing orders to correct them. The Captain is the benevolent, all-knowing Good Guy, and the hated XO is the knee-breaking enforcer of the Captain's command vision. Okay, I was an Executive Officer, I get it. But the responsibilities of the job should never be an excuse for a small-minded, weak officer to flex his authority and issue unwarranted abuse on the crew just to make himself feel powerful.

My Guided Missile Frigate had one of those petty tyrants with a chip on his shoulder as XO. A Naval Academy graduate, he had suffered a bad fitness report (Fitrep) in an earlier command, and so was very much behind the professional eight ball. In the hyper-competitive officer culture of the 1980s Navy, Fitrep grade inflation was a simple fact of life. To ever have a hope for promotion and/or command selection, every officer had to have PERFECT marks on all Fitreps. One or two grades below "A" on any Fitrep would consign the officer to never selecting for command afloat, and possibly to never achieving promotion beyond the grade of LCDR (0-4). One or two "B"s were the professional kiss of death.

This XO was in that situation, and he was taking steps to try and overcome his deficiencies by riding roughshod over every aspect of this crew's daily life. He was hoping to blaze such a trail of excellence in the ship's administration, appearance and discipline that the Captain would take notice, write him the mother of all excellent Fitreps, and eclipse the offending marks on his record, making him able to select for command and continued promotion.

The problem was, this XO was obese, and a poor leader. He loved to enforce standards which he himself did not meet on all other crew members with ruthless zeal. He thought that telling the Captain how screwed up his officers were, and what he personally was doing to correct their work, thereby helping the ship shine, was a surefire way to earn the Captain's love. And he heaped cutting sarcasm and verbal abuse about in liberal fashion, with little chance of receiving any payback due to his rank and position. But sailors have their ways of getting revenge.

One day, the ship was entering port in Pearl Harbor. Typically, when entering a port that is not your home, a ship's crew changes from shipboard working uniforms into service dress uniforms. We were resplendent in Summer Whites. As Navigator, I was working with my team of Quartermasters at the Bridge chart table, piloting the ship safely into the harbor. My Navigation Assistant was a Senior Chief Quartermaster (E-8). This guy was excellent in every way. He was a great leader, a superb navigator and a genuinely nice guy. I relied upon him heavily to teach me my trade and to tell me when I was about to do something that would not serve me or the ship well. He was my most trusted enlisted mentor. He was also something of a character. He had spent much of his career as a Navy diver. Divers tend to be a fairly rough-hewn bunch of bare-knuckle sailors, who live in an extremely demanding and practical world and who brook no BS. To give you some kind of idea what this guy was like, he had two tattoos of old-style cross-handle faucets, one on each breast. One was labeled "Sweet" and one "Sour." He had only returned to shipboard Quartermaster duties after he left dive status a few years earlier.

The XO had previously been stationed on a cruiser in Subic Bay, Philippines, and when he had gotten orders to my ship, he had gone into town and ordered himself a beautiful, custom-made navy blue ball cap with the ship's name and silhouette and his job title embroidered on it. It was unique and he wore it proudly every day in working uniform as he cut his trail of destruction through the ship. On this day, the XO changed into his whites, and donned his matching combination cover hat. For some reason, he felt it appropriate to walk over to the chart table and make several cutting and sarcastic remarks to the Navigation team about some imaginary infractions, heaping undeserved abuse on us while we were busily engaged in our important work. And he flung his treasured ball cap onto the chart table right in the middle of our plotting and calculations, turned his back and stalked away.

This was too much for the Senior Chief. His expression turned dark, and he grabbed the ball cap by the bill and made a pantomime of throwing it out the bridge wing door. I smirked and said "Oh, yeah. Right, Senior Chief. You ain't gonna do that."

The Senior Chief's eyes blazed and bugged out. Then he turned smartly on one heel, strode out the door to the bridge wing, and chucked that SOB over the side. It spun lazily in the ship's wake, filled with water and sank into the depths of Pearl Harbor, joining countless other relics of failures of naval leadership.

My mouth dropped open, and with eyes as big as portholes, I looked at him and said **"Holy S#%&! Senior Chief!"** Still furious, he looked back at me and said **"Well, you shouldn't have dared me then!"** We went back to work.

Hours later, after the ship was moored, the XO waddled up to the bridge to retrieve his ball cap. "Sorry, sir. Haven't seen it. Must have gotten moved when the Bridge was secured after Sea Detail."

The moral of the story? "Don't piss off the Senior Chief!"

The End

ACKNOWLEDGEMENTS

Across my brief and undistinguished naval career, I was privileged to serve and sail with a number of remarkable men, all of whom stand as shining examples of the very best and most important of the U.S. Navy's assets: her excellent sailors. Very few of the thousands of men and women who serve in the Navy and Coast Guard meet the bar of excellence set by these wonderful shipmates. Each was a tough, skilled professional and each served our nation with distinction for as long as they chose to wear the uniform. They taught me much, supported me in times good and bad, suffered and exulted with me, and traveled afar at my side. They were the kind of shipmates with which a man, knowing they are on watch, sleeps soundly. I wish to express to them all my most heartfelt appreciation. They already command my undying respect.

In alphabetic order, in the rank they held when I served with them:
GMG1 (SW) Carmine Accordino
LT N. A. "Andy" Catlett
LTjg Jerry Doherty, USCG
OSC (SW) / ENS Joseph Farrell
LCDR F.M. "Mac" Garrison
CDR Myron "Mike" Gray
MSC (SW) David Handley
LTjg Keith Herchenroder, USCG
ENS Thomas Jennings
LT Bradley F. Jublou
QMCS (SW/DV) Richard Julin
LTjg Richard McElroy
LT W. Scott McKay
LT Brian G. McKeever
LTjg Dan McCleod, USCG
LT Leo L. Mingle

BMCM (SW/DV) Calvin C. Piper
CWO3 Terry Priestley
ENS Charles W. "Chip" Rock
GSM2 (SW) Don Schuler
LT Larry Seeley
CDR Kenneth D. Slaght
OS2 (SW) Steven Strasshofer
BMCS (SW) Gilbert R. Swearingen, Jr.
LT Ross D. Telson
RADM M.E. Toole
LT Daniel Waterman

Fair winds and following seas, my friends. God bless you all.

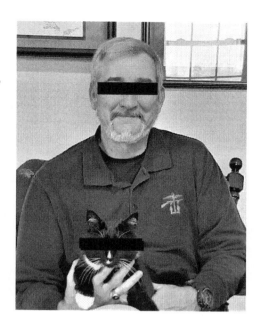

"Kim Kipling"

ABOUT THE AUTHOR

"Kim Kipling" (a pseudonym) is a retired U.S. Navy officer and CIA Paramilitary Operations Officer. He received his commission in 1982 from the NROTC, and served on active duty as a Surface Warfare Officer from 1982-1990. While serving afloat, he crossed swords with several superior officers. Predictably, this severely limited his upward career mobility. After leaving active duty, he remained in the Naval Reserve and retired as a Lieutenant Commander in 2003. He enjoyed a thirty-plus year career with the Central Intelligence Agency, which values competence and candor more than the U.S. Navy does and has a higher tolerance for reasoned (and correct) dissent. He lives in Tennessee, with a three-legged tuxedo cat with the heart of a lion.

Made in the USA
Columbia, SC
28 June 2022

62394598R10141